Especially for

....

From

....

Date

....

How God Grows a Woman of Wisdom

A Devotional

Anita Higman &
Marian Leslie

BARBOUR
PUBLISHING

Published by Barbour Publishing, Inc., 1810 Barbour Drive, Uhrichsville, Ohio 44683, www.barbourbooks.com

Our mission is to inspire the world with the life-changing message of the Bible.

Printed in China.

Lovingly dedicated to
Richard and Michelle Modisette.
You are blessings to this world!

Anita Higman

To my mother, my mother-in-law,
and all the other wise women who have
so graciously poured into me.

Marian Leslie

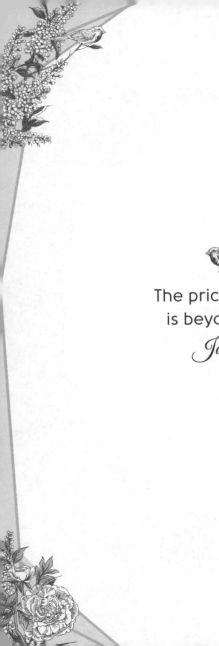

The price of wisdom
is beyond rubies.

Job 28:18

Introduction

It's easy to dismiss *wisdom* as an antiquated biblical term. It sounds so foreign to the modern mind-set, maybe a little lofty, and almost unattainable. But to God it's a spiritually discerning way of living that never goes out of style. It's as vital as air is to our lungs.

Wisdom isn't about someone's IQ or how many degrees one has. Wisdom is the perceptive and godly judgment that keeps a woman on track. Keeps her moving forward in grace, beauty, and love. A woman of wisdom is a woman of prayer, faith, and strength—a woman everyone admires.

Where can we get such a beauty treatment for the heart? Since God is the Father who loves to give good gifts to His children, all you have to do is ask. . . .

The Way of Heaven

*There remains, then, a Sabbath-rest for the people
of God; for anyone who enters God's rest also rests
from their works, just as God did from his.*
HEBREWS 4:9–10

People have become a blur. We spend our lives racing from place to place, barely able to breathe. We have great intent but little purpose. Sometimes the only thing to slow us down is a severe health issue or death. Why do we wait for disaster to slow us down? Probably because the wild winds of the world beckon us to whirl forward in our careers, our agendas—to make the most of every hour, every minute. Even on Sunday.

But that's not the way of God. He has another vantage point—the one from heaven. We humans are not machines; we are flesh—and spirit. We cannot go and go without collapsing. We need respite, refreshment, repose, and reflection. If the God of the universe felt it was important to rest after His labors in creating our earth, how much more vital is it for us frail beings to give up our labor one day each week?

One of the Ten Commandments tells us that Sunday is more than a day of rest; it is also a holy day. So let us worship our Lord on Sunday. Let us put up our feet. Let us be refreshed for a new week of loving and being loved.

That is the way to live—that is the way of heaven.

*God, You know what's best for me. Help me
to follow in Your ways. Amen. —AH*

My Sweetest Delight

"Come to me, all you who are weary and burdened, and I will give you rest. Take my yoke upon you and learn from me, for I am gentle and humble in heart, and you will find rest for your souls.
MATTHEW 11:28–29

A yoke doesn't make one think of a happy frolic in the meadow, but of some kind of heavy oppression. So much of the time that is the way we see life—as oppressive. But God's Word promises us a reprieve when we stay near Him.

The refrain from the old hymn, "His Yoke Is Easy" by Daniel S. Warner goes:

> His yoke is easy, His burden is light, I've found it so, I've found it so; His service is my sweetest delight, His blessings ever flow.

But even more stirring are two of Mr. Warner's verses to the song:

> My flesh recoiled before the cross, And Satan whispered there, "Thy gain will not repay the loss, His yoke is hard to bear."

> I've tried the road of sin and found, Its prospects all deceive; I've proved the Lord, and joys abound, More than I could believe.

Yes, so true. Satan's finest hour holds nothing but deception and despair. But even in God's discipline, we discover mercy. Even when He allows struggles, there is joy!

Jesus, thank You for giving me rest and new life. Free me from my burdens. Amen. —AH

All of These Rhapsodies Are Ours

The Lord replied, "My Presence will go with you."
EXODUS 33:14

Think of the most scrumptious meal. The most romantic sunset. The cuddliest pet. The most irresistible perfume. The most passionate love. The most achingly exquisite melody. All of these rhapsodies put together dim in comparison to one flashing, spellbinding moment in the Lord's presence. After all, He is the one who created these delights, either directly or through humans gifted to produce them.

When it comes to God's presence, we think too small, too finite. It's as if we're focused on a dirty penny fallen inside the sewer grate when all the beauty and wonder of the world is ours if we only gaze upward—if we bask in the presence of God. Look up to the heavens and grasp a more profound picture of the "who" of God. He is small enough to be inside your heart, and yet He is vast enough to rule the universe. He is beyond our understanding, and yet He wants to have a relationship with you—an intimate bond of friendship. Imagine. We are so dear to His heart, in fact, that He said His presence will go with us.

So ask for His nearness in your life. Sit at the foot of the Master and be ready for redemption. Be receptive to love. And yes, be prepared to be staggered in awe.

Father, You are the origin of all richness, joy, and love. Help me to seek You every moment of every day. Amen. —AH

The Foot of the Matterhorn

The LORD is my shepherd, I lack nothing. He makes me lie down in green pastures, he leads me beside quiet waters, he refreshes my soul.
PSALM 23:1–3

Between Italy and Switzerland, not far from the base of the Matterhorn—which is one of the most spectacular peaks in the Alps—there are ponds and lakes sublime enough and wreathed in grasses verdant enough to have inspired David's words in Psalm 23 when he writes, "He makes me lie down in green pastures, he leads me beside quiet waters."

But you don't have to travel great distances to find bodies of water like this. They are in abundance around the globe, and God, in His wisdom, will make full use of them. Of course, God can refresh us while we're waiting at a traffic light on a busy street corner with blaring horns, but there is something about relaxing by the shore, listening to the waters lap, gurgle, and ripple away again, that gets into our souls and allows us to better hear that still, small voice of God.

There by those golden shores, those quiet waters, the Lord will work out the kinks in our spirits. He'll prompt us to release what we thought we had under control but didn't. He will remind us how He treasures us, how He loves us, and how He pursues us more diligently than a lover.

Lord, please refresh my spirit, and help me to rely solely on Your guidance. Amen. —AH

Just as Sure as You Draw Breath

Be still before the LORD and wait patiently for him;
do not fret when people succeed in their ways,
when they carry out their wicked schemes.
PSALM 37:7

Did you ever have your day planned out to perfection, just to have it completely decimated? The source of your undoing might be a friend, a relative, or a coworker. Or it could even be someone you share a pew with at church. It's not your imagination—just as sure as you draw breath, there is someone out there scheming against you. She might have good intentions or might not give a flying fig that she made your plans unravel like a ball of loose twine bouncing with wild abandon down the stairs. That is the nature of a fallen humanity.

But God has a few words for us on the matter: stop fretting about it.

Even if a fellow sojourner means us ill, we can commit that person to the Lord. We can let God handle our affairs. We can even sit back and wait patiently for Him. How hard is that? In our humanness, it is virtually impossible. Yet in God's power, everything is possible. And no matter what the situation looks like from your end—no matter how much a fellow human being may think he or she has power over you—never forget, the Lord has the ultimate authority, the utmost power, and the final say in your life. Praise God!

Father, help me to remember that You are always
watching over me. I have nothing to fear. Amen. —AH

He's Whispering Your Name

"Peace I leave with you; my peace I give you. I do not give to you as the world gives. Do not let your hearts be troubled and do not be afraid."
JOHN 14:27

You know the feeling. You're sweaty. You're heart is beating outside your chest. You're scared out of your mind. It's like a panic attack on steroids, a nightmare that you can't wake up from.

It's called life.

What's a body to do? According to the Bible, there's plenty you can do. But there's only one voice to listen to. Can you hear it? It's God's, and He's whispering your name. He's saying, "Don't be troubled. I have been waiting for you. Run to Me. My arms are open wide. I will hold you every step of the way. Never succumb to fear. The worries of the day and the terrors of the night are ploys from the enemy.

"Perfect love hurls your fear into the pit of hell where it belongs. The world has no peace to give. It is as sturdy as paper, and its promises fade. The peace I offer is hand-molded and divinely cured. It's usable, durable, and beautiful. It is forever."

*Lord, help me to make a home in the stronghold of Your love.
I don't want to rely on this world for my comfort or fulfillment.
You are my sustenance and my purpose. Amen. —AH*

How Should I Talk to God?

Do not be anxious about anything, but in every situation, by prayer and petition, with thanksgiving, present your requests to God.
PHILIPPIANS 4:6

When you hear the words, *an anxious heart*, what do you think of? Perhaps a hummingbird's fast heartbeat, which can beat 1,260 times per minute? Or an animal that paces back and forth restlessly in its cage with no hope of escape?

When we become nervous, and we feel trapped and alone, there's a simple explanation—we have forgotten how to pray, how to trust. Fortunately, God gives us some excellent guidelines on prayer. In fact, Jesus gave us an example of how to pray in His famous petition that was recorded in Matthew 6:9–13:

> "This, then, is how you should pray: 'Our Father in heaven, hallowed be your name, your kingdom come, your will be done, on earth as it is in heaven. Give us today our daily bread. And forgive us our debts, as we also have forgiven our debtors. And lead us not into temptation, but deliver us from the evil one.' "

We don't need to suffer with an anxious heart or feel ensnared by this world with no one to hear our cry for help. We can talk to God, right now, and He will listen. The act of prayer is as simple as launching a boat into the Sea of Galilee, but it's as miraculous as walking on water.

God, how wonderful it is that You hear me when I call out to You and that You answer with exactly what I need. Amen. —AH

That Dress Is So You

---

*But the LORD said to Samuel, "Do not consider his
appearance or his height, for I have rejected him. The LORD
does not look at the things people look at. People look at the
outward appearance, but the LORD looks at the heart."*
1 SAMUEL 16:7

Have you ever been shopping when the fashion planets seem to
align perfectly and your friend gasps and says, "That dress is so
you"? Perhaps she means it fits well, it's complementary to your
figure, it makes you look younger or smarter, or it brings out your
skin tone or the color of your eyes. When that magical moment
happens, we feel victorious. Nothing wrong with that. Buy the
dress—enjoy the day.

However.

Just to keep things in perspective, the fashion industry cares
only for the outer woman. That is, it's not interested in how God
wants to grow us into women of beauty from the inside out. Our
true essence and "look" should come from the knowledge of who
we are in Christ, not from a designer label. If we follow Christ
with a whole heart, our reflection will be far more stunning than
the finest haute couture, and that light and beauty will radiate
and forever change a dark and hurting world. Yes, clothes are
fun and necessary, but they shouldn't "make" the woman. That's
the business of God.

*Jesus, help me to remember that my worth isn't
defined by my outward appearance. Transform me
daily into a greater likeness of Yourself. Amen. —AH*

A Masterpiece in the Making

*"For I know the plans I have for you," declares
the LORD, "plans to prosper you and not to harm
you, plans to give you hope and a future."*
JEREMIAH 29:11

When we're in the midst of trials, we can become so focused on the details of our miseries it seems impossible to see the bigger picture—the divine plan. Life is a little like a mosaic, and we spend way too much of our time seeing only the tiny stained pieces that we place into the wall of our lives.

As the Master Craftsman, God can take those oddly shaped and mismatched fragments of this fallen world—of our lives—and make something beautiful. He can take what sin has wrought, what Satan has perverted, and what man has meant for evil, and create a grand and glorious picture.

So the next time people tell you that life is random and ir-redeemable, without a plan, a hope, or a future, step back from the world's view, and behold what others refuse to see—witness a masterpiece in the making.

*God, help me to trust in Your perfect plan, even when
I don't understand it. You are sovereign and all-knowing.
I have no reason to fear because You are in control.
I place my life in Your hands. Amen. —AH*

God Is Doing Something New

"See, I am doing a new thing! Now it springs up; do you not perceive it? I am making a way in the wilderness and streams in the wasteland."
ISAIAH 43:19

So much of life depends on the flow of thirst-quenching water. Creeks, streams, and rivers draw people to congregate and build towns around them and to plant crops that grow into fields of harvest. On the other hand, to experience a dearth of water across the land can be devastating. It can make a verdant valley inhospitable. It can make what seems like a promise perilous.

Imagine that desert, dry and barren—with no hope of even a cactus flower to bloom—suddenly coming to life with bubbling pools of pure water. That is what God promises us. He is doing something new in our lives. He is making a path through what feels impassable, and He will command a stream to flow through the wilderness of our pasts, places where we had only known the wasteland of sin and a landscape of despair.

So believe in what God can do. Have faith, and bring your empty buckets to the stream. Lift the dipper to your parched lips, and taste the water that is sweet and new and refreshing.

Father, thank You for Your provision, hope, and joy. Without You, life is dry and hostile. Come into my life and quench my thirst. You are the only one who can fulfill me. Amen. —AH

We Have the Keys to the Vault

"You are the light of the world. A town built on a hill cannot be hidden. Neither do people light a lamp and put it under a bowl. Instead they put it on its stand, and it gives light to everyone in the house. In the same way, let your light shine before others, that they may see your good deeds and glorify your Father in heaven."
MATTHEW 5:14–16

Christians sometimes cower around nonbelievers as if we only have trinkets of truth to offer the world. But God is the Creator of all things. He is the Alpha and the Omega—the beginning and the end—who is, and who was, and who is to come. What the Almighty has to offer, no other god can give. God's gift of salvation through Christ is awe inspiring, unmatchable, eternal.

We as followers of Jesus have the keys to the vault, inside of which are the most beautiful riches ever seen. No earthly king, not even Solomon in all his glory, could offer such gems as forgiveness, redemption, and eternal life.

Let us unlock the vault, swing open the doors, and let the world see what we have—*who* we have. Christ is beautiful and without flaw, so much so that He can pour pure light into every dark crevice of this fallen earth. So let this truth and light kept in the treasury of our hearts shine before everyone!

Jesus, help me to represent You and light the way for others in this dark, fallen world. Thank You for Your saving grace. Amen. —AH

What Is Our Defense?

Our struggle is not against flesh and blood, but against the rulers,
against the authorities, against the powers of this dark world
and against the spiritual forces of evil in the heavenly realms.
EPHESIANS 6:12

Sometimes when people talk about the dark spiritual forces mentioned in the Bible, the words sound so otherworldly, as if they're reading the script of a fantasy movie. If we haven't witnessed the powers of darkness—demons—it's easy to believe they don't exist. But according to the Bible, they, a legion of angels that fell with Satan when he defied God, are very real.

Since our struggle includes what we cannot see, what is our defense? In Ephesians 6:13–17, the apostle Paul tells us to. . .

> put on the full armor of God, so that when the day of
> evil comes, you may be able to stand your ground. . .
> Stand firm then, with the belt of truth. . .the breast-
> plate of righteousness. . .with your feet fitted with
> the readiness that comes from the gospel of peace.
> In addition. . .take up the shield of faith. . .the helmet
> of salvation and the sword of the Spirit, which is the
> word of God.

Those directives sound like a battle cry—and they are! There is a war going on in the spiritual realms—it's a fight for your soul.

So be watchful, and stay devoted to Christ who loves you and gave His life for you. Then, like Paul, you can say in that last hour, "I have fought the good fight, I have finished the race, I have kept the faith" (2 Timothy 4:7).

Lord, You are my strength and protection. Defend
me from evil, unseen forces. Amen. —AH

Seeing Others through "God Glasses"

Therefore, as God's chosen people, holy and
dearly loved, clothe yourselves with compassion,
kindness, humility, gentleness and patience.
COLOSSIANS 3:12

Your boss got a raise because he stole all your best ideas, your dearest friend of ten years can't seem to remember your birthday if her life depended on it—not even an e-card—the line at the post office is held up because of a woman at the front counter who can't stop jawing about the sweater she knitted for her poodle, and solicitors' calls interrupted supper three times. So realistically, how can anyone be clothed in compassion, kindness, humility, gentleness, and patience every hour of every day? It's just not possible. Humans are too annoying!

We can't do anything on our own. But if we ask the Holy Spirit to help us, He will be faithful and provide a way for us to flee from those urges to lash out at people. To react in the flesh. He'll help us to see others through "God glasses"—that is, seeing people the way they were meant to be and what they still *can* be in Christ.

Ask the Holy Spirit for "God glasses." It will forever change the way you see other people, and the way you see yourself.

Holy Spirit, give me new eyes so that I can see others
as God sees them. Help me to love as Christ loves—
without selfishness or limit. Amen. —AH

Good Reason to Smile

*Surely your goodness and love will follow me all the days of
my life, and I will dwell in the house of the LORD forever.*
PSALM 23:6

If we wear a scowl, we can keep the whole world at bay, but with
a smile, people will surely turn our way. It might even change their
day! Okay, it's a corny little rhyme, and yet there is truth in it. How
many times have you been in a foul mood and someone gave you
a smile—a big, gooey, genuine, glad-to-see-you smile—and it
turned your heart the other way? So much so, you smiled back.
Then maybe you gave someone else a smile later on since you'd
recovered some of your groove.

So what happens next? Perhaps the smiles have a rippling
effect, and they travel all around the city. Maybe your smile will
defuse somebody's stink bomb—the one she was going to drop on
some poor, unsuspecting coworker later in the day. The person you
disarmed might ask you what you have to smile about in such a
grim-faced world, and she might even listen to what you have to
say. So put on that happy face. After all, if the goodness and love of
the Lord is following us all our days, and we are to live in the house
of the Lord forever, we have good reason to share, to shout, and
to celebrate. And at the very least, we have good reason to smile.

*Heavenly Father, help me to be always mindful of my
eternal home and to spread the boundless joy and peace
that comes from that knowledge. Amen. —AH*

Living in the Now

*But one thing I do: Forgetting what is behind
and straining toward what is ahead.*
PHILIPPIANS 3:13

Regret isn't always bad—it can lead us to repentance. But once we've repented, we sometimes let the guilt of already pardoned sins build back up like a pile of trash. Even though we've been forgiven, we go back out to the street, lift the garbage lid—wince, of course, at the stench—and then proceed to pick through old sins as if God wasn't capable of taking away the refuse of our transgressions.

We want to help Him out. Dig through things. Lift them up one by one, and stare at their smelly, raggedy carcasses. We choose to feel the shame all over again. And maybe through this unbiblical act, we believe we've done God a good service by feebly attempting to help Him absolve our iniquities. Yet our paltry efforts, our lack of faith, declare that the sacrifice Christ made with His very life wasn't enough.

In the meantime, while we're picking around in the rubbish like wild animals at a garbage dump, we aren't able to live in the present and we too easily disregard our future—which is exactly where the enemy wants us. Burdened. Joyless. Unusable.

Let us agree together to allow Jesus to remove the rubbish of our past sins, once and for all, and rejoice in a clean heart. Praise God. We can indeed live in the now, and we can celebrate the future!

*Jesus, may I never forget the power of Your
sacrifice on the cross. Amen. —AH*

The Sweet Aroma of Reconciliation

"Therefore, if you are offering your gift at the altar and there remember that your brother or sister has something against you, leave your gift there in front of the altar. First go and be reconciled to them; then come and offer your gift."
MATTHEW 5:23–24

God is into fragrances. In the Old Testament there are a number of places where He speaks of a pleasing aroma coming up from man's sacrifices on the altar. In the New Testament, Jesus was deeply moved by the woman who poured expensive perfume on His feet. When people reconcile, surely it puts off a sweet scent like none other, one that wafts and curls its way up to heaven, one that makes God smile.

But reconciling with someone requires a humble attitude on our part. That is, coming to terms with our dark side—the little hiding places of resentment, and pride, and a host of other emotions that don't put off such a lovely smell.

Putting things right means approaching someone who may be angry and confused. It means taking time to talk things through in love, having to say we're sorry. But it also means we won't have to carry the burden of that grudge any longer. We'll have a lighter spirit. Less baggage. More room for God.

May we always be ready to open that bottle of reconciliation and let its pleasing scent flow into our hearts—and then onto our lips.

God, please give me a humble heart so I can make amends and let go of grudges. May every area of my life be pleasing to You. Amen. —AH

Which Way Do I Go?

I will instruct you and teach you in the way you should go; I will counsel you with my loving eye on you.
PSALM 32:8

Conversationwise, there are two kinds of folks in this world—the kind who are better at listening and the kind who are better at talking. Hmm. Which one are you? If you're better at listening, then your friends, boss, and spouse must *really* love you!

Listening is important in all kinds of relationships, even the one with God. He is the master of all listeners, but God also has something to say, and you can be assured that whatever He has to tell you, it's worth listening to.

God's words of wisdom might be about your future. So much of the time people feel as though they're floundering, not really knowing where to go or what to do next. But God says, "I will instruct you and teach you in the way you should go; I will counsel you with My loving eye on you." That is truly what we need in a noisy world that may offer little reliable or usable advice. God not only promises to guide us, to teach us the way we should go, but He plans on doing it with a loving eye on us. That sounds irresistible.

So for the most loving counsel, listen to the voice of God. He's talking to you, and He has something important to say that will change your life.

Wonderful Counselor, help me to be receptive to Your voice and to always trust in Your guidance. Amen. —AH

The Mission Bell Rings

For God so loved the world that he gave his one and only Son,
that whoever believes in him shall not perish but have eternal life.
JOHN 3:16

The locust is an insect that is feared in many parts of the world. That small, seemingly innocent-looking bug will come in a swarm, and that cloud of pestilence will descend upon a field, wiping out an entire crop. A year's worth of living. Gone. Such needless destruction. Such massive loss.

That is so reminiscent of the way sin affected the Garden of Eden. The first couple listened to Satan, defied God in open rebellion by eating what was forbidden, and fell into decay. Such a seemingly innocent piece of fruit caused such great destruction. Such loss. The collapse of paradise. But in this story of mankind, God intervenes. He wanted to make a way. To rescue people from the devastation of their choice—the ruins of their sin. So He sent His Son, Jesus.

Have you ever embraced Christ as the one who is without sin, who took yours so that you could be free? Why not? There's no reason to hesitate. No need for delay. The hour of your redemption has come. The mission bell of your heart is chiming, ready to acknowledge Him as the Savior, the greatest lover of mankind, the glorious "I Am." Open the door and take Him into your arms. For all time.

Sweet Savior, thank You for enduring the pain
of the cross and for taking on my sin so that I can
enjoy all of eternity with You. Amen. —AH

A Word of Encouragement

A cheerful heart is good medicine.
PROVERBS 17:22

Instead of a cheerful heart, a sincere smile, and a word of encouragement for the nonbeliever, some Christians arrive on the scene with the black tar of judgment and the feathers of condemnation. These believers seem almost in a fit of gleeful anticipation, hoping for a chance to tar and feather some poor souls to show them just how wicked they are. It's not the most uplifting way to live one's life or the most fruitful method of winning folks to Christ.

Not only is a cheerful heart good medicine for our souls, but it's a good way to win over someone who's not known the love of Christ. Your joy may not make non-Christians come running to Christ, but it will make them curious to know more about who He is and why He came.

So the next time we have a chance to witness, to share what Christ has done in our lives, let us all wear a winsome smile, carry a humble attitude—rather than a big stick—and pass along a merry heart. We can leave the sour censures, the sanctimonious stance, and the Scrooge-like countenance for a Dickens play come Christmastime.

God, help me to accept others as You accepted me. How can I possibly judge when You alone are the Source of my righteousness? Guide and sustain me as I extend Your love and grace to the world. Amen. —AH

27

Jesus Is Asking, "Do You Trust Me?"

Those who know your name trust in you, for you,
LORD, have never forsaken those who seek you.
PSALM 9:10

Shakespeare said, "Love all, trust a few." That statement holds some wisdom. It is right and good to love everyone. As Christians we are called to do that very thing, yet trust is a very different matter.

Who can we trust? Lots of people are reliable when it comes to small things, but when it comes to the serious stuff—the long-term commitments that require steadfast devotion—well, that's where the rubber meets the road, doesn't it? And some people aren't all that steady and dependable. They flop around in the ruts of life like wobbly flat tires.

There's no getting around it. Sometimes people fail us. Friends may abandon us. Spouses may commit adultery. Coworkers may gossip. And neighbors might snub us for no good reason at all. The book of Psalms tells us that it is better to trust in the Lord than to put confidence in man. True. In a world that is fickle and disloyal, Jesus is the one constant. He will never leave us or forsake us. No matter what we've done or where we've been, Jesus is the dependable one who keeps us moving forward.

Jesus is asking, "Do you trust Me?"

My Redeemer, help me to rely fully on Your
grace, provision, and love. Thank You for being
steadfast and always present. Amen. —AH

On Easter Morning

There was a violent earthquake, for an angel of the Lord came down from heaven and, going to the tomb, rolled back the stone and sat on it. His appearance was like lightning, and his clothes were white as snow. The guards were so afraid of him that they shook and became like dead men. The angel said to the women, "Do not be afraid, for I know that you are looking for Jesus, who was crucified. He is not here; he has risen, just as he said. Come and see the place where he lay."

MATTHEW 28:2–6

A child's eyes light up when she's given a basket decorated for Easter. Pastel ribbons and a nest of softness, just waiting for its pretty colored prizes. A few of her important questions are: *How many eggs are hiding in the grass? Will there be candy inside? Will I find a bunny too?* How wonderful to see a child animated with excitement, surprise, and wonder. She is bursting with enthusiasm, unable to contain her joy.

As Christians on Easter morning, we have every reason to feel all of those emotions. We have every reason to light up with excitement and wonder. We should be bursting with enthusiasm, unable to contain our joy. After all, we have the best surprise of all. The best hope of all.

We have an empty tomb.

Father, thank You for the hope of Easter morning. May that elation be always on my heart and mind. Amen. —AH

The Gaze of Pomposity

There are six things the LORD hates, seven that are detestable to him: haughty eyes, a lying tongue, hands that shed innocent blood, a heart that devises wicked schemes, feet that are quick to rush into evil, a false witness who pours out lies and a person who stirs up conflict in the community.
PROVERBS 6:16–19

You can spot egocentric people across a crowded room at any party. They have this upward tilt to the chin, a few extra glances as they pass by a mirror, the puffing of the upper body, the oozing of self-possession, and that unmistakable condescending tone of—haughtiness.

But it won't do any good to point a finger at them, because somewhere down the line, we've all been guilty of this offense. It's an easy sin to commit, and yet it's not acceptable. In Proverbs, when it comes to the character qualities that God hates the most, haughtiness tops the list.

Let's face it. Many folks are suffering from the spiritual ailment called king-of-the-mountain syndrome. Sitting up too high from the rest of humanity, we're blinded to the people who need us. We lose sight of all that is important in this life and the life to come. We're trying to be God rather than be used by Him.

So what can save us from this egotistical pit? A good start is knowing that everything we are and own is from God. Every brain cell we use to impress, all the material wealth we flaunt. Every beat of our heart and breath we take is a gift from His hand. It really isn't all about us. It's about a relationship—with God.

Lord, forgive me for all the times I made too much of myself instead of You. Amen. —AH

The Diadem of Beauty

LORD, our Lord, how majestic is your name in all the earth! You have set your glory in the heavens.
PSALM 8:1

God is the Light of the world, the diadem of beauty, the King of kings, and Lord of all. He is a wall of fire. No man can hold Him back. He is the Vine. All of life that is good flows through Him. He is Truth. All wisdom can be found in Him. He is the Fountain of living waters. He is the Gentle Whisperer, the Good Shepherd. He offers what no other god or angel or human can—redemption through Christ.

And yet we've heard God's name said frivolously, used as a curse word, and abused in a hundred different ways. But God remains awesome in spite of what man thinks or says or does. We cannot change the nature of God. We cannot dim His radiance. We cannot diminish His power. But we do have the freewill to decide who He is, who He sent to rescue us, and what place He'll take in our hearts.

Each of us has a choice to make—the most important decision we'll ever make.

Who is Christ to you?

Awesome God, You are the Author of all creation and truly worthy to be praised. Make a home in my heart so that my every thought, action, and word will reflect Your wonderful character. Thank You for allowing me to have such a close, intimate connection with You. Amen. —AH

Divine Imaginings and Sublime Aspirations

He has made everything beautiful in its time.
He has also set eternity in the human heart.
ECCLESIASTES 3:11

Do you ever wake up in the morning, groan at life, and then turn over and go back to sleep? Do you ever think maybe you were meant for more than what the day will bring? That the many tarnishing factors of life have begun to corrode your outlook? Most of us have felt that disintegration of heart—that decay of mind, body, and spirit.

And yet. . .

We were created for so much more—for divine imaginings and sublime aspirations, for beauty and love and life. For sweet laughter. We were made for communion with the Most High.

Let us wake up knowing that even though we exist in a fallen world, we can have the assurance that God has bigger dreams for us than we imagined. We have every reason to wake up with our toes wiggling and our spirits dancing, to begin our day asking God, "What shall we do today, Lord? Will we change the world, You and me?"

Let's join hands. Let's celebrate. God has made everything beautiful in its time. He has also set eternity in the human heart. Never sit in the gutter when the steps of paradise are at your feet! So widen your scope. See beauty in all things, great and small. Soar free. Imagine beyond the ordinary. Love large. Forgive lavishly. Hope always. Expect a miracle.

Father, give me a contagious enthusiasm for life.
You have given me everything I need. Amen. —AH

Let Me See What You See

Make the most of every opportunity.
COLOSSIANS 4:5

We can be certain that if God tells us to make the most of every opportunity, He's not just talking about our career planning and our financial portfolio. He's also talking about being sensitive to the stirring of the Holy Spirit when it comes to those encounters that might alter someone's steps, which might point a fellow sojourner toward the kingdom.

These opportunity portholes might appear all day long, but if we are too occupied, too riddled with worries, too whirling with our own thoughts to see those fleeting moments, we will miss them altogether. Those inspired moments might arrive as a chance to encourage someone who was about to fall into depression, or the opportunity to make a casserole for the elderly neighbor who's just come home from surgery, or it might be the right moment to offer the story of salvation to someone who is drifting through life, lost.

The moments are there, and they have our names written all over them. So ask the Holy Spirit, "Please let me see what You see. Let me be courageous enough to follow through with those divine appointments that could change a life. Let me carry Your light and offer Your cup of cool water—Your living water—to this weary and heartbroken world."

It only takes a moment to change a life—to be a blessing.

Holy Spirit, be the voice in my ear that inclines me to do good and to love much. Amen. —AH

Just Because

*Love the LORD your God with all your heart and
with all your soul and with all your strength.*
DEUTERONOMY 6:5

Kids love receiving presents from their parents, whether it's Christmastime or their birthday or for no reason at all. They adore fun activities and special treats of every kind. Yes, for kids, goodies and fun surprises reign supreme. And parents like giving their children good gifts, whether their kids are two or thirty-two. It's in a parent's nature to do so. But sometimes a parent might wonder what would happen if the goodies ran out. Would the kids still come around? Would they still want to spend time with Mom and Dad? Would they still care? Parents want to know that their kids love them, just because.

Perhaps God wonders the same thing about us. We like God when all is well, when life is flowing and the presents are plentiful, but it must make Him sad to think that we might not need Him or love Him as much when the good times and the gifts dry up. Do we still trust Him? Are we still able to love the Lord with all our heart and soul and strength? Or do we doubt, grumble, and fuss like small children?

God delights in His children, and He loves giving them good gifts. It's in His nature to do so, and yet He wants to know that His kids love Him, just because.

Do you?

*Father, help me to love You with all of my heart, soul, and
strength in every circumstance—good or bad. Amen. —AH*

A Hallelujah Moment

At that moment the curtain of the temple was torn in two from top to bottom. The earth shook, the rocks split and the tombs broke open. The bodies of many holy people who had died were raised to life. They came out of the tombs after Jesus' resurrection and went into the holy city and appeared to many people.
MATTHEW 27:51–53

When Jesus is around, big things happen. People are changed. Dead people come back to life. Even the earth cannot remain silent in His presence as the rocks split and the earth trembles.

Our response to Christ's death, resurrection, and daily presence in our lives should be one of praise and worship. By now most people have heard the "Hallelujah Chorus," from Handel's *Messiah*. If you've experienced this masterwork in a big auditorium with a large audience, you know that there is a thundering sound when everyone rises from their seats to honor the majesty of the music written to honor Christ.

With that song one can almost hear the thunder that rumbled across the earth on that monumental day when Jesus gave Himself up to die on the cross for us. Because of that willing sacrifice and because of His miraculous resurrection, He is praiseworthy. He is awe inspiring. He is marvelous. He is beautiful. The Kings of kings and Lord of lords. With Christ, every day is a hallelujah moment!

Mighty King, Your glory and majesty are beyond compare. Help me to worship You all the days of my life. Amen. —AH

Living the "What If" Blues

And we know that in all things God works for the good of those
who love him, who have been called according to his purpose.
ROMANS 8:28

Looking at our past choices and trying to foresee the future can be like staring into two different black holes. We don't know for sure what could have been had we taken a different path, nor do we have any idea of what may await us. All this "not knowing" can prompt a lot of what-ifs.

What if I'd gone to college? What if I'd married Derek instead of Dudley? What if I'd gone into interior design instead of accounting? What if I'd stayed in touch with my sister before she passed away? And as far as the future, what if I say the wrong thing to my boss and get fired? Or buy the wrong house or move to the wrong city? Our lives are full of these questions, which can drive us mad if we let them.

What to do?

Pray for wisdom and guidance, knowing that God will give them to you freely and lovingly. But if you still take a wrong turn, embrace His promise that He will work all things for good for those who love Him. Hard to imagine, but the Lord really does mean "all things." Praying and embracing His promises will go a long way in keeping you on the right road, as well as easing those "what if" blues.

God, I'm so grateful You can turn evil into
good and sorrow into joy. Amen. —AH

It Will Happen Like This

*For we know that if the earthly tent we live in is destroyed,
we have a building from God, an eternal house in heaven,
not built by human hands. Meanwhile we groan, longing
to be clothed instead with our heavenly dwelling.*

2 CORINTHIANS 5:1–2

It'll happen like this. You'll be staring into one of those big lit magnifying mirrors—the kind that highlights every possible wart, gray hair, and crinkle—and you'll suddenly notice that your lower lip isn't attached as securely as it used to be. I can tell you, there's no amount of Elmer's that's going to fix that problem.

It's called aging.

Our earthly tent isn't what it used to be. In fact, one can even say that about every human at any age. But the good news is that as Christians, someday we will be transformed. We will have bodies that we recognize, but they'll also be ones that don't lose their beauty or health or ever experience any loose parts. We will be better than we've ever been or ever imagined.

In the meantime, we groan with this sore and sagging earthly flesh, yearning to be draped in our heavenly attire. But that great day will come. So think on that when you stare a little too long into that ghastly magnifying mirror. Know you will not need to live in this aging body forever. God makes all things new, including you!

*Lord, thank You for the hope of a heavenly dwelling. Give me
strength and comfort in my present struggles. Amen. —AH*

Only a Prayer Away

The Lord was pleased that Solomon had asked for this. So God said to him, "Since you have asked for this and not for long life or wealth for yourself, nor have asked for the death of your enemies but for discernment in administering justice, I will do what you have asked. I will give you a wise and discerning heart, so that there will never have been anyone like you, nor will there ever be."
1 KINGS 3:10–12

What is *wisdom* exactly? The dictionary might define it as good sense. One could easily say that wisdom is an earthly commodity that is always needed but in short supply. When Solomon became king he asked God for wisdom. The Lord was so pleased with the boy's request that He gave him great wealth and honor too.

Oh, to walk in wisdom. It would make life less stressful and more enjoyable. We'd have fewer regrets, know when to speak, when to be silent, and how to respond to people and the daily barrage of problems that come our way. We'd have discernment to make sensible decisions that people respect. Doesn't that sound amazing?

If Solomon can ask for wisdom, so can we. James 1:5 reads, "If any of you lacks wisdom, you should ask God, who gives generously to all without finding fault, and it will be given to you."

In obtaining wisdom, the asking and the receiving are only a prayer away.

Father, give me the wisdom I need to live a
life that is pleasing to You. Amen. —AH

The Showroom Floor

Take delight in the LORD, and he will give you the desires of your heart.
PSALM 37:4

When you think of God giving us the desires of our hearts, it's easy to conjure up certain visions. Such as a child in a candy shop, ordering a bag of every kind of sweet in the store. Or a woman strolling through a five thousand-square-foot model home and saying, "I'll take it. . .all of it." Or perhaps a man who sees a sports car, red and loaded with every option imaginable, and then drives his dream vehicle right off the showroom floor.

These longings may not be too far from reality, and having desires in the material world isn't necessarily wrong. However, Psalm 37:4 reveals the fact that the promise of heart-desires met is connected to our delighting in God, a caveat that may seem foreign to us.

What could it mean to "take delight in the LORD"? To find pleasure in and seek out His company. To spend time talking—and listening—to Him. To discover His friendship, His fellowship, and laugh with unexpected delight, as if we'd indulged in the finest riches that earth had to offer. When we delight in God, all the treasures of earth dim in comparison. The world offers mere diversions and fleeting amusements compared to His presence!

So delight yourself in the Lord. Life can't get much better than that.

Father, You are my greatest treasure, my deepest joy, and my brightest hope. Amen. —AH

Hidden from Man, Visible to God

May these words of my mouth and this meditation of my heart
be pleasing in your sight, LORD, my Rock and my Redeemer.
PSALM 19:14

Humans have the unique ability to use words to convince people that we adore them, all the while entertaining some not-so-adoring thoughts about them. Well, we might be able to fool friends, relatives, strangers, even church folk, but we can't fool God. He knows our innermost meditations, the pretty ones as well as the ugly. And we might as well own up to it.

Proverbs 23:7 says that whatever a man thinks in his heart, he is. If our inner life is contaminated with sour and spiteful thoughts, then they stain our entire being. The mark may not stand out to the world, but it's there all the same, soiling our spirits and sullying our relationship with the Lord.

Maybe what we need is a good spring-cleaning of our minds. Let's pull up the shades, throw open those painted-stuck windows, and allow the Lord's sweet searching and convicting presence to waft through. Ah, feels better already.

God, please forgive me for my unkind thoughts about others.
Help me to view everyone with Your grace and love. Purify
my mind and spirit with Your gentle touch. Amen. —AH

The Lion of Judah

Oh, the depth of the riches of the wisdom and knowledge of God! How unsearchable his judgments, and his paths beyond tracing out! "Who has known the mind of the Lord? Or who has been his counselor?"

ROMANS 11:33–34

Religiously, we are a tidy folk. We like to put all our spiritual truths in little boxes that will fit nicely upon the shelves of our desires and needs, likes and dislikes, limited wisdom and knowledge, and human prejudices. We like to place God in one of those boxes too. But He will not fit. Not even close. How can a Creator who is so mysterious, unfathomable, and magnificent be placed in an ordinary box that was made by a finite mind? It is like the goldfish telling the whale that he, the small goldfish, knows the vast depths of the seas!

If we cannot know the whole of the universe, how can we expect to know the Creator of that universe? No matter how advanced civilization claims to be, we will never be able to control an omnipotent God. We cannot hem or rein Him in. We cannot wholly know His mind and methods since His ways are not ours. Praise God for that. We don't want a god who can be easily contained, controlled, or categorized. We need a God who is the Lion of Judah, not a docile kitten we can play with when we choose to.

We may not fully understand the Almighty, but, through Jesus, we can get to know Him and His love.

Creator God, I am in awe of Your vastness, wisdom, and mystery. Amen. —AH

41

Make Music to Him. Shout for Joy!

Sing joyfully to the LORD, you righteous; it is fitting for the upright to praise him. Praise the LORD with the harp; make music to him on the ten-stringed lyre. Sing to him a new song; play skillfully, and shout for joy. For the word of the LORD is right and true; he is faithful in all he does.

PSALM 33:1–4

When the choir leader asks members of the congregation to stand, they generally do. But when he tells them to sing unto the Lord, they sometimes just mouth the words.

You know who you are.

Why do we feel a need to raise our voices in excitement and laughter for every reason imaginable—including sporting events—except in praise to God?

If God is in your life, sing and shout His praises. If He has proven to be faithful and good, tell the world. Don't be silent. Sing a new song for Him. Make music for your Lord. Do it well—"play skillfully," He says—and with your whole heart. It is fitting for the upright to praise Him. For the word of the Lord is not only right—but true! He is faithful in all ways. He deserves our devotion.

So what song do you have in your heart that needs singing? What news do you have to share? What miracles and blessings do you want to shout about?

The Lord longs to hear you, and the world is dying without it.

Father, may my worship of You be genuine, constant, and contagious. Amen. —AH

42

The Elusive Butterfly
of Contentment

*I am not saying this because I am in need, for I have
learned to be content whatever the circumstances.*
PHILIPPIANS 4:11

What is it to be content?

Just as soon as we think we see it—that gladness of heart—settling on our shoulder like a butterfly, it flutters away. This usually happens after we hear about our friend's new car, or find out about our neighbor's new promotion, or see our coworker's new wardrobe. The list really could be as long as this book and still not cover all the things we might covet, things that could snatch away our contentment.

What do we think we'll gain from wishing and striving for more and bigger and better? God expects us to work, and a good day's labor is commendable, but no matter what material blessings we have, there will always be someone who has more. Always.

In 1 Timothy 6:6–8, Paul says, "Godliness with contentment is great gain. For we brought nothing into the world, and we can take nothing out of it. But if we have food and clothing, we will be content with that." With today's money-grubbing mind-set, that scripture sounds like a hard climb. Actually, contentment is impossible without the right point of view—that is, the one from heaven. There will be no striving in heaven for material gain and glory, since then we'll be able to see earthly treasures clearly for what they are—more fleeting and fluttery than a butterfly—but not nearly as beautiful.

*Gracious God, remind me that it is from You alone
that I find true contentment. Amen. —AH*

Safe in His Dwelling

For in the day of trouble he will keep me safe in
his dwelling; he will hide me in the shelter of his
sacred tent and set me high upon a rock.
PSALM 27:5

Trouble looks like that black horse of Revelation 6:5, thundering toward us. It comes bearing bad tidings, bringing fearsome days and sleepless nights.

Life is full of those black horses. The Bible calls a time of darkness "the day of trouble" (Psalm 27:5). When the doctor has bad news. When a friend dies unexpectedly. When you're fired from your job without reason. When you lose your retirement money in a poor investment. When adultery shakes your marriage to its core. The black horse of trouble and despair can come at any time.

But the good news is that we are safe when we rest in Jesus, when we run to His dwelling place. He will not turn us away but will care for us as His precious ones. God may not sweep away all the trials from this life, but He will be near us. He will never fail us, and He will bring good out of all we endure. This is our hope and promise until He takes us to be with Him, where there will be no more pain, hunger, tears, disease, war, or disasters. Never again a day of trouble. Only light, love, and joy.

But until that new heaven—trust, know, rest.

You are safe in His dwelling place, hidden in the shelter of His arms.

Lord, thank You for Your boundless protection
and provision in my darkest hours. Amen. —AH

No Wallflowers Here

*She is clothed with strength and dignity; she can
laugh at the days to come. She speaks with wisdom,
and faithful instruction is on her tongue.*
PROVERBS 31:25–26

What would the ideal woman look like? One of the Stepford Wives? The perfect wife might please man, but a noble woman pleases God. And Proverbs 31 really gives a great overview of what she would look like. She isn't fragile and mealymouthed—no wallflowers here—but strong, poised, and respected for her gracious attitude. She is welcoming, and her house feels like home to everyone who enters.

A godly woman can laugh at the future, because her trust rests in God, not in man or circumstances. She can assess the past and learn from it, but she is sensible enough to live in the present, where she can be useful. She is so wise that people come to her for advice—and take it.

So how can any woman measure up to these high standards? It's never going to be easy, but it is doable—with Christ. By staying in His Word. Memorizing scripture so you can come against the enemy just as Jesus did. Attending a Bible-believing church. Fellowshipping with other believers. Praying without ceasing.

A Proverbs 31 woman is far from boring—she is a woman of substance. A woman everyone wants to know. A woman who's easy to love and impossible to forget.

Are you a Proverbs 31 woman?

*Father, help me to become the kind of woman who can shed Your
light and love on others and point them to You. Amen. —AH*

Preferred Provider

Praise the LORD, my soul, and forget not all his benefits—
who forgives all your sins and heals all your diseases, who
redeems your life from the pit and crowns you with love
and compassion, who satisfies your desires with good
things so that your youth is renewed like the eagle's.
PSALM 103:2–5

Is anyone ever really comfortable in a hospital? Perhaps some—maybe those who work there daily, scrubbing floors, attending to patients, pushing carts of medicine from door to door. But in most hospital hallways the air is thick with anxiety. And why not? There, on the tiled floors and between the calm-colored walls, there behind sterile curtains and antiseptic sheets, there live all the things people fear the most—sickness, pain, grief, death. . . and health insurance.

But even the grimmest of these fears need not overcome those who trust in the Great Healer. He brings light to the darkest shadow cast on the sick patient's face. He breathes comfort into a crowded waiting room. He delivers peace through the gentle, skillful hands of nurses, doctors, and loving caregivers.

It is a normal human reaction to want to avoid situations that make us squirm with discomfort or that reveal hearts and bodies as the fragile things they are. But running from these moments physically and doubting God spiritually exposes us to an even greater risk—missing all the benefits of the greatest health-care Provider of all.

Great Physician, remind us to put our trust in Your
perfectly capable hands, and help us to see all the ways
You heal us, over and over again. Amen. —ML

Blown Away

Then we will no longer be infants, tossed back and forth by the waves, and blown here and there by every wind of teaching.
EPHESIANS 4:14

Can you imagine walking along the beach, peering out over the ocean, and seeing a bunch of babies bobbing on the waves? But that alarming and absurd scene depicted by Ephesians 4:14 is not so far off from what plays out on most TV and computer screens in any given week—especially when some controversial topic ("wind of teaching") hits the headlines. Have you noticed how many people seem to have unprecedented access to the mind of God these days? Ten minutes surfing on the Web and you could find that God wants us to save the dolphins and kill crocodiles, make peace and arm for war, buy more and spend less, and to take up a whole host of other contradictory and confusing positions.

As usual, Paul brings clarity: "Make every effort to keep the unity of the Spirit through the bond of peace" (Ephesians 4:3). Our goal, in our actions and in our words, should be to "reach unity in the faith and in the knowledge of the Son of God and become mature, attaining to the whole measure of the fullness of Christ" (Ephesians 4:13).

And maybe Paul's point here is, if you haven't yet reached that level of maturity, don't go swimming in the ocean.

Dear God, help me to hear Your voice clearly and follow its sound when so many others are shouting. Help me to grow and become what You made me to be in the Body of Christ. Amen. —ML

Pretty Ugly

Like a gold ring in a pig's snout is a beautiful
woman who shows no discretion.
PROVERBS 11:22

Well-manicured nails, trendy hair, cute designer clothes, lovely skin, and a perfect size-6 figure. Oh, and one more thing—a mouth that will not shut up.

You've seen her. Maybe you know her. Or possibly—gasp!—you are her. The girl who dishes gossip up like gourmet, hand-churned ice cream, who vandalizes reputations with words faster than you can say "graffiti," who can't keep a secret to save anyone's life. And no amount of lipstick can make that ugliness disappear.

A gold ring in a pig's snout is all wrong in at least two ways. First, no amount of gilding is going to turn that slimy, muddy, wrinkly snuffler into a lily. The valuable gold just goes to waste when put in such an unattractive place.

Second, that ring is likely put into the pig's snout as a tool to help lead the pig around. Perhaps here lies a secret message. Maybe the proverb writer is telling us that not only will the woman's beauty be lost by her unwise actions, but she may lose what power she thinks she has as well. The woman who is so foolish as to run her mouth off will soon be led by the nose.

Almighty God, help me always remember that
every word I say has consequences. Help me not
to lose control of my tongue! Amen. —ML

Pondering

But Mary treasured up all these things
and pondered them in her heart.
LUKE 2:19

Everyone loves to have a good story to share—well, maybe not *everyone*. Mary had one amazing night. She gives birth in a stable, angels provide the birth announcement, and a bunch of smelly shepherds show up as her Baby's first visitors. A birth story to rival any other for all time, that's for certain.

But instead of running around and telling anyone who would listen about her incredible experience, she stays quiet. She "treasures up" all these happenings and ponders them. What must she have been thinking? Was she afraid for her infant Son's life? Was she concerned about who might show up next? Was she planning for His college education?

We know from her song (see Luke 1:46–55) that Mary had a humble heart: "My soul glorifies the Lord and my spirit rejoices in God my Savior, for he has been mindful of the humble state of his servant" (verses 47–48). Instead of worrying over what might come next or eagerly planning to tell all her friends and relatives about giving birth to the Lord of lords, perhaps Mary was just cherishing this chance to cuddle with her little one, and to thank God for the wonder of it all. Maybe she was practicing the art of being still and knowing that He is God.

God, when amazing things happen to me, help me to
remember to give You the glory first before I open my mouth
to tell the story. Help me to value what You have to say to
me more than the sound of my own voice. Amen. —ML

Straight Paths

*"Make ready the way of the Lord, make his paths straight
. . . The crooked will become straight, and the rough roads
smooth; and all flesh will see the salvation of God."*
LUKE 3:4–6 NASB

Stand at the beginning of a crooked road and it's hard to see much past the first turn. Stand at the head of a straight road and you can see which way it's headed, right from the first step.

For many of us, the path to God is not straight. We experience deep valleys of trouble, worry, suffering, depression, and similar hardships. A walk with Jesus is no walk in the park. But the more we learn about God, the more we know Him, the easier it is to see the direction of the road stretching out in front of us—leading straight to our place at His feet.

So how can we possibly "make his paths straight," when we often can't see straight ourselves? As sinful creatures, we struggle with sticking to any one path at any given time—except perhaps the path of least resistance. But even John the Baptist didn't have to be perfect to "make ready the way of the Lord." He just pointed people in the right direction.

To do that, we have to "produce fruit" (Luke 3:8). We have to take actions that show we are on the path to God, that we are following in the footsteps of Christ. That means taking care of other travelers as well, and helping them find their footing. As we do more for others, we think less about ourselves, and that is one big obstacle that disappears, making rough roads smooth.

*God, help me not to be a bump in anyone's road.
Help me to point the way to You. Amen. —ML*

Because He Says So

*"Master, we've worked hard all night
and haven't caught anything."*
LUKE 5:5

It's been said a million times: No one gets anywhere without hard work. But what about when hard work isn't enough? Or when you've worked your hardest, and you still fail?

Jesus has the answer. But you're not going to like it. No one ever does. It's the one thing we find hardest to succumb to, the one piece of advice that will make the eldest among us plug her ears like a small child, the one path we will walk the longest around and fall the farthest from in order just to avoid it.

Obedience.

After a very long and unsuccessful night, the fishermen were washing their nets—bitterly getting rid of all the flotsam and jetsam they had collected, instead of fish. And then the Teacher calls over to them, telling them to try one more time.

Simon was doubtful. "But because you say so, I will let down the nets" (Luke 5:5).

And the fish nearly jumped right into the boats. It's no wonder why Simon then proclaimed his shame. We know what he'd have been thinking—*This Rabbi doesn't know anything about fishing.*

But the One who was present at the creation of the fish of the sea does know. So when He sits down in our boats with us, and tells us what to do—no matter how many times we've tried before or how hard we think we've worked—the only wise thing left to do is obey.

Because He says so.

Lord, bend my will to Yours. Amen. —ML

Not So Sacred

"Why are you doing what is unlawful on the Sabbath?"
LUKE 6:2

Those poor Pharisees. It was bad enough they had to deal with what this renegade Rabbi said, but now His followers were daring to do actual work on the Sabbath—rubbing heads of grain in their hands. When would this madness end?

Jesus doesn't give them a straightforward reply to their question, "Why are you doing what is unlawful on the Sabbath?" Instead He reminds them of what their king David did once: he ate the sacred bread. The tension must have been visible on the faces of those religious leaders right at this moment, because you know what they were probably thinking: *This Jesus person wouldn't dare do that, would He?*

But Jesus was just trying to drive home a point. That bread was not so sacred. The temple building itself is not so sacred. This business about not being allowed to do the "work" of feeding oneself a handful of grain on the Sabbath? Not God's idea.

What's your not-so-sacred thing? Is your life run by rules that God did not give? Do you get irritated when someone messes with the way things have always been done at your church? Or in your home?

Every once in a while, it's good to take a step back and examine the set of unwritten (or written) "rules" we are living, working, and worshipping by. Are they from God? Or not so sacred?

Oh God, Rulemaker for us all, please bring to my attention times when I take pride in things that are not of You. Open my ears to Your Word, and help me not to judge others. Amen. —ML

Speechless

When words are many, transgression is not lacking,
but the prudent are restrained in speech.
PROVERBS 10:19 NRSV

How many words does it take to get into trouble? Sometimes it's only one: *yes*.

But most times, on the heels of trouble, come more words—streams of gushing guilt, giant vats of justification and equivocation, spouts of spite and stress, and bitter rivers of regret. We use words to hurt those who want to help us, to find reasons for our wrongdoing, and to blind our enemies. . .and our friends.

Think of the last time you did something wrong. Maybe it was losing your temper with your kids or ridiculing the driver in the next lane or lying a little about what you did last weekend. If you regretted it, you've probably had to cough up words of apology to someone. If you haven't admitted to yourself it was wrong yet, you're probably still developing different ways to tell your side of the story.

"The prudent are restrained in speech." Not just because it's wise to do more listening than talking, but because the prudent don't have to talk so much. If you make wise choices, you don't have to do so much damage control.

So save your vocal cords. Give yourself a breather. After all, sometimes it only takes one word to avoid getting into trouble: *no*.

God, please help my choices to be wiser and
my words more worthwhile. Amen. —ML

Begin at the Beginning

"The fear of the LORD is the beginning of wisdom,
and the knowledge of the Holy One is understanding."
PROVERBS 9:10 NKJV

Children's first lessons come from the basis of our fears for their safety, which in turn, instills fear in them. Don't touch—it will burn you. Don't run across the street—you may get hurt. Don't answer the door—it's not safe. Don't talk to Mommy before she's had her coffee—now *that's* terrifying!

This is not nightmare-producing fear (except for maybe that last one). This is not the kind of fear that makes your skin crawl, gives you goose bumps, or makes you want to cry.

This is smart. This is sensible. This is respectful.

But to have healthy fear and learn from it, you have to know who to fear. For example, you should not fear the words of that paid spokesman on the shopping channel who insists you are going to die in seven days if you don't take his supplement. Neither should you fear every article writer on the Internet. Nor buy into the latest trend—short shorts and tank tops are not for everyone. Trust me.

But when you get to know God, who He is, what He does, and what He has done for us, the knowledge of the Holy One brings an understanding that cannot be clearer. The fear of the Lord is not bad. The fear of the Lord is beautiful, enlightening, exciting, challenging, and good. And that's a great place to start.

God, help me to always start with You. Amen. —ML

The Worrier's Psalm

Do not fret.
PSALM 37:1

Do not fret. Just don't.

Don't fret because people are evil. People do bad things. They have since the beginning of the world, and they will to the end of it. Worrying about it is not going to make them stop.

Don't fret because people who do wrong seem to get away with it. Their day is coming.

Don't fret, because worrying leads to bad decisions. Don't make choices based on unhealthy fear. Don't fret, because anxiety too quickly becomes anger.

"But fretting is what I do," you say. "It's who I am!" Then you need a new you. A you who trusts in the Lord. A you who waits patiently for what God is going to do. A you who can "hope in the LORD and keep his way" (verse 34).

Instead of fretting, delight in the Lord, and He will give you all your heart's desires.

Especially if one of those desires is to be free from fretting.

And even if you've prayed, breathed, tried to relax, and the worries still come, like houseflies that just refuse to find their way back out the screen, then don't fret about fretting.

Trust. Commit. Be still. Wait. Refrain. Turn. Give generously. Lend freely. Do good. Hope. Consider. Observe. Seek peace. Just don't fret.

Dear God, You know our hearts and the worries that prey on our minds. Please help us to stay busy doing good and to grow in trust and patience. Please help us to let go of control we never had to start with. Amen. —ML

The Nearness of You

Come near to God and he will come near to you.
JAMES 4:8

This verse has a pleasant sound to it. Something like a love song. One could imagine oneself cozied up in God's embrace, safe and secure in the loving arms of our forever Friend.

But James is no romantic. Here's what he tells us to do *after* we come near to God: "Wash your hands, you sinners, and purify your hearts, you double-minded. Grieve, mourn and wail. Change your laughter to mourning and your joy to gloom. Humble yourselves before the Lord, and he will lift you up" (verses 8–10).

Kind of kills the mood, doesn't it?

All of that sounds so hard, so painful. So we think there must be a better way.

"Come near to God," we hear. And we think, *I can do that.* So we take up our notebooks and buy the most inspirational Bibles complete with ribbon bookmarks and study notes, we create quiet-time nooks, we go sit under trees, we spiritually retreat and . . .find we are no closer. We don't feel closer to God; we feel tired.

So we follow the rest of James' instructions. We pray, we pour our hearts out, and maybe even cry. We humbly admit our faults to God. Finally, James says, "*Now*, you've got it!" Because it was never about us making ourselves any better. We are messed-up people. Even our best efforts at doing better are going to get us nowhere in the end. Once we humbly admit that fact, God will lift us up. And *that's* how we get nearer, by realizing we can't do anything without Him.

My God, my Friend, my Lover, my Savior.
Humble me, so You can lift me up. Amen. —ML

All Too Familiar

"God, I thank you that I am not like other people."
LUKE 18:11

Have you ever said this prayer? Or one like it? "Thank God, we aren't that bad." "Good heavens, I'm glad no one I know is like that!" "Well, we might not be perfect, but at least we've never _____!" (Fill in the blank with an appropriate sin.)

The Pharisee, one of the two men who went up to the temple in Jesus' parable, is the infamous author of this prayer. But it's doubtful he meant any true gratitude. His actual thoughts would have gone something like this: *If I could have everyone's attention, I would just like it to be noted that I am one of the best citizens around: generous to a fault, an upholder of the law, and extremely disciplined. If anyone would like to know more about being holy, I'll be taking questions after this presentation.*

Perhaps you've never said such words, or even thought them, but could it be that you have, somewhere in a small corner of your mind, felt just a little bit better than other people? A little more worthy? A little more deserving?

Jesus sets us straight. It was the other guy who "went home justified" (Luke 18:14). The tax collector. The guy who wouldn't even look up. The guy who stood at a distance, beating the words out of his chest, "Have mercy on me, a sinner" (Luke 18:13). The two prayers could not have been more different. The two prayers? They had a lot in common.

God, if I ever start thinking of myself as better than someone else, show me the truth. Amen. —ML

57

Family Picture

---

*How wonderful, how beautiful,
when brothers and sisters get along!*
PSALM 133:1 MSG

You've probably seen some awful family photos. Ones where you just know the mom tried *so hard* to get everyone looking nice and sitting still for just ten seconds, but even that ten seconds was too much to ask. Brother pulls sister's hair, sister sticks tongue out at brother, fingers point in accusation, someone gets knocked over, someone's feelings get hurt, tears, bruises. . .anarchy.

Not that you have personal experience, of course.

What do you think the church's family picture would look like? If we could somehow manage to get all the people in all the congregations around the world to sit still and look nice for just ten seconds, what would happen? Would the photo be all lovely and Olan Mills perfect? Or would it show fingers pointing in accusation, someone getting knocked over, someone's feelings getting hurt, tears, bruises. . .anarchy?

It's highly unlikely we can do much about the world's Christian population in general, but what can we do in our own communities to make a better family photo? What can we do to become a better family?

Pray to promote peace, love, and unity between our brothers and sisters, beginning with ourselves.

*Dear God, let me be an instrument of Your peace.
Help me, in whatever conversations or relationships I develop,
to build up unity among Your followers. Amen.* —ML

Doing

Never tire of doing what is good.
2 THESSALONIANS 3:13

Women are often accused of doing too much. Sometimes it seems frenetic activity is the only thing that keeps us from falling over. We are birthday-party planners, car-pool drivers, exercisers, group leaders, and caregivers. We are mothers, stepmothers, sisters, daughters, grandmothers, aunts, cousins, wives, and friends. We organize, prioritize, separate, combine, mix, cook, sew, embroider, embellish, clean, rinse, wash, and repeat. We create, play, think, write, plan, schedule, meet, run, start, and finish.

And we get tired, doggone it! And that's okay.

When Paul was writing his letter to the Thessalonians, he wasn't writing to a bunch of idle folk. These were people he thanked God for. Timothy gave a good report about these men and women because of their faith and love. These were good, hardworking people.

But Paul urges the Thessalonians to not confuse being busybodies with being busy. He urges them to do good work so they may earn the food the community shares with them, not a gold star or an employee-of-the-month award.

Sometimes doing good means doing a lot. And sometimes doing good means not doing much. It's listening to someone while conversing over coffee or taking care of a kid with a cold. Sometimes it is taking a nap. Don't give up doing, but remember to rest. And make sure that what you are doing is good, and not just doing.

Lord, help me to have the energy and spirit to do what is good for Your kingdom. And when I am tired, refresh my soul. Amen. —ML

Loneliness

"Yet I am not alone, for my Father is with me."
JOHN 16:32

There are many shades of loneliness. When friends have been visiting, and then go away, the silence that comes is stained with their absence. When someone you live with every day has to leave for an extended time, the ache of missing him colors everything you do. When a dear friend dies, the hole she leaves behind highlights details you never noticed before.

But the gray sorrow that comes from not being known, from feeling stuck where no one understands you, is a dense shadow that threatens to block out all light.

Jesus' words to His friends, as He tried to tell them of the events to come, are heavy with this kind of loneliness. It seems the weight of the sins of the world was already bearing down on His shoulders. He felt the separation to come—not just the separation from those who truly loved Him but the separation from His Father God that would come as Jesus hung on the cross.

Who could understand our loneliness better than this Man? It is no wonder He is called our Counselor, that He is known as Immanuel—"God with us." When we feel all alone in the world, there is no one who can be truly with us like Jesus can: "I have told you these things, so that in me you may have peace. In this world you will have trouble. But take heart! I have overcome the world" (John 16:33).

Dear Jesus, thank You for being with
me when I feel all alone. Amen. —ML

Tempting Truth

*Because he himself suffered when he was tempted,
he is able to help those who are being tempted.*
HEBREWS 2:18

Satan's lies to the human race boil down to three kinds, with one goal in mind. Lie #1: You are worse than everyone else. Lie #2: You are better than everyone else. Lie #3: No one has been through what you are going through.

And the goal? Separation.

It's the old game of divide and conquer. If our enemy can get us to divide up into smaller groups, indeed into the smallest groups of all, it will be far easier to destroy us.

There are many words in the Bible, whole books even, that tell us the truth about these lies. Hebrews 2 is one of those chapters that stands out. There, we learn Truth #1: We are not so bad—"a little lower than the angels" (verse 7). Truth #2: We are not so good—only Jesus is the one made "perfect through what he suffered" (verse 10). And Truth #3: Jesus does know exactly what we are going through, because He was made "fully human in every way" (verse 17). There is no one who will win the you-won't-believe-what-I've-been-through contest except the Son of God, aka the Son of Man.

So much for separation anxiety. And what mercy our Father shows us! He designed a plan to let us know and be known by our Creator in the only way that would work to help us defeat Satan's well-crafted lies.

*Lord God, Thank You for Your amazing mercy and
grace, and for revealing to us the only truth that can
squash the lies of the deceiver. Amen. —ML*

Rights

Not everything is constructive.
1 CORINTHIANS 10:23

When the Spice Girls hit the pop scene in the mid-nineties, "girl power" suddenly became much more than a fashion trend. While there's no doubt that young girls need encouragement and support and confidence, for Christians, there's more at stake here than women's rights.

Paul makes the condition of things clear in his letter to the Corinthians. " 'I have the right to do anything,' you say—but not everything is beneficial. 'I have the right to do anything'—but not everything is constructive" (v. 23).

Little girls need to be made to feel strong because they have been designed by a strong God who loves them and wants them to stand up for what is right. But no member of the body of Christ should buy into the idea that she has the right to do anything simply because she is a human being.

As Paul states, "No one should seek their own good, but the good of others" (verse 24). Paul delivers this message to the Corinthians over and over again in his letters—no man (or woman) is an island. As followers of Christ, we are part of one body, and as part of that body, we have a duty and a responsibility to take care of one another, from the youngest and weakest one of us, to the oldest and strongest.

And that duty trumps any other kind of individual power every time.

Dear Father, as women of God, help us to be strong and supportive of one another and to put others' needs before our own desires. Amen. —ML

Care

You may have seen shows about so-called stupid criminals. They're the guys who get easily caught in their crimes, usually through a series of poor decisions on their part. It's the guy who parks his getaway car in a towing zone, or the one who decides to steal from a place where they have his name and address on a database.

Surprisingly, it's not so much a lack of intelligence that is the problem for these ill-fated felons. It's not that their enemies are supershrewd or that the criminals get overpowered. It's not a tendency to violence, a psychological problem, or a drug addiction either. The heart of their problem is complacency. They stop caring. Or they become so confident, they think they don't need to care anymore.

So they are careless. And they do care less. And less. And less. Until one day, it destroys their lives. What small plans for a future they once had crumble apart. The people they used to depend on disappear.

Wisdom calls out to us in Proverbs. She tries to help us out: "Whoever listens to me will live in safety and be at ease, without fear of harm" (verse 33).

The message of Proverbs 1:32 isn't just for the very wicked or not very bright. There's not a single one of us reading these words right now who can claim she has never let complacency rule the day. But if you're honest, you'll admit that, at some point, the act of not caring cost you more than it was worth.

Dear God, help me to keep on caring, every day. Help me to care for others as much as You care for me. Amen. —ML

The Sole of Discretion

Discretion will protect you,
and understanding will guard you.
PROVERBS 2:11

In the summertime, some people go a little wacky. This is revealed in their footwear fashions. Gone are the clunky boots and water-proof gear of winter. Out come the fabulously tall high heels, the brightly colored flip-flops, and the sandals that hardly can be called footwear at all—just a bit of string and cardboard.

It may be fun to try out different shoes, but when it comes to actually getting anywhere, good, strong walking shoes are neces-sary to provide your feet with the protection and support they need.

In a similar way, discretion is a requirement for protecting your soul. This protection goes two ways. First, the act of being discreet saves you from revealing too much about yourself to others who may not care what they do with your personal information. Second, discretion keeps you from saying things that might hurt your relationships with others.

Chatting, swapping stories, and sharing bits of our lives—that is often how good friendships are formed. But keeping others' secrets quiet, protecting honest reputations, and building trust are how good friendships are kept.

If you're headed to the beach for a swim, slip on the fun, care-free flip-flops. But if you're going out for a long walk, you'll need something more solid.

Dear God, help me to be wise every
time I open my mouth. Amen. —ML

Guarded

Above all else, guard your heart,
for everything you do flows from it.
PROVERBS 4:23

Be careful. Young women, you who have not yet promised your lives in marriage to someone, be careful in the vows you make. There is no shame in slowness here. Before you give your word or make a commitment, or break one for that matter, think hard. Think for a long time. Imagine your life based on the choice you are to make. Then when you've done all that and are sure of your answer, wait a few days more.

Be careful. Married women, you who have already said your vows and given your hands, be careful about becoming complacent. Decide to love your spouse each day. And decide to guard your heart each minute. Don't get wrapped up in fairy-tale visions of what you thought would happen or what your life might be like if. . . Be present, right now, where you are, with the person you are in covenant with. This is serious business. Treat it that way.

Be careful. Women who have been divorced or widowed, be careful that you don't sell your heart for cheap. You are worth as much today, if not more, as you were on the day of your wedding. Don't let loneliness eat away at your joy. Be mindful of what your experience has taught you—don't ignore those lessons for passion. Respect yourself, respect your friends, respect your God.

Be careful. Everything you do comes from your heart. Guard it with your life.

Lord Jesus, help me to realize the value of my heart
and to treat it as the precious thing it is. Amen. —ML

Enough

Don't love money; be satisfied with what you have.
HEBREWS 13:5 NLT

Be satisfied. It sounds so easy, so simple. Right? Just be that way.

Open your closet doors and your dresser drawers. You have enough. You don't need another shirt or skirt or pajama bottom.

Open your makeup bag or your medicine cabinet. You have enough. You don't need another lip gloss or a Botox injection (who needs that?).

Open your pantry and your refrigerator doors. You have enough. You don't need to shop in the fancy gourmet food store. You don't need another piece of chocolate. (Unless it's been a really bad week. . .)

Look out toward where you keep your car or bike, or pick up your bus. You have enough. You don't need a shinier chariot. You don't have to have an easier way.

Now go look at your most recent stack of bills. You have enough.

Maybe you are drowning in debt. Maybe you've already sunk. Maybe you have more than enough. God asks us to be content.

No one loves money, really. We love what it can get us—freedom, status, identity, a place to be, ability, and mobility.

But God doesn't want us to look to money for these things. He wants us to look to Him. "I will never fail you. I will never abandon you" (Hebrews 13:5 NLT). You have enough. God says so.

Dear God, help me not to worry about what I don't have and to be content with and grateful for everything. Amen. —ML

On the Way

*Start children off on the way they should go, and even
when they are old they will not turn from it.*
PROVERBS 22:6

Listen up. This message is not just for parents. It's for anyone who
teaches a child, knows a child, loves a child, cares for a child, sees
a child on a regular basis, or may someday do any of these things.
It's also for anyone who has ever been a child.

This is the most important piece of parenting advice on the
market: start them as you mean them to go on.

That's all.

If you want them to be loving, kind, caring, and good, surround
them with love and kindness, care and goodness.

If you want them to be bold, creative, thoughtful, and challenging, build them up with questions, encouragement, projects,
and goals.

Because you better believe it can go another way.

Start children off on the wrong path, and it will be a struggle
for them to change. Start them off in pain, fear, fighting, and
strife, and they will live their lives with their fists up. Start them off
with abuse, hatred, deceit, and neglect, and they will live their
lives always grasping for what they cannot have.

So pay attention. Watch out for the little ones around you. You
never know what your small interaction with a child might do for
her day, or her life.

*Dear Father of us all, help us to understand the value
of the precious little lives around us. Amen.—ML*

Teach Them All the Time

Teach them to your children, talking about them when
you sit at home and when you walk along the road,
when you lie down and when you get up.
DEUTERONOMY 11:19

Of all the commands laid out in the book of Deuteronomy, this must be one of the most daunting. Why? Because to obey it, you don't need a lesson plan, you need a lifestyle.

Children are little sponges and parrots. They are remarkable creatures—spongy parrots. They soak up our words, our mannerisms, our traditions, and our routines, then imitate everything we say and do. It's pretty scary, really.

And to learn, children need exactly this kind of repetition and reinforcement. To really take a thing to heart, they have to be exposed to it every day, in multiple forms.

So you can see where this is going. If you are living with a child and want that child to learn about what God has done for you, and what God wants us to do, then you have to talk about God when you get up and get breakfast. You have to act like you know God and try to do what He says. You have to tell stories about Him, pray to Him, and thank Him for the day when you tuck your child in at night.

And to do that, you have to know God really well. Clever plan on God's part, isn't it?

Dear Lord, help me to study Your Word and take it to heart, so I
can pass it on to my children or any children I know. Amen. —ML

In the Fishbowl

Live such good lives among the pagans that, though they accuse you of doing wrong, they may see your good deeds and glorify God on the day he visits us.
1 PETER 2:12

There may be people in the world who enjoy being followed and watched every minute of the day. But most of us would prefer privacy.

However, if you are a known follower of Christ, your life is on display, whether you like it or not. People will watch you. And people will wait for you to make a colossal mistake.

This message from Peter makes this painfully clear—even when you are living right and trying to do your best, someone is going to say you're doing something wrong. Fingers will be pointed. Criticism will be posted.

But if you can just keep it up, if you can keep going, keep serving, keep loving, keep trying, the reward is amazing. In verse 15, Peter says, "For it is God's will that by doing good you should silence the ignorant talk of foolish people." Isn't that a beautiful thing? Could there be any silence more golden than the one that shuts the mouths of the lions through your own good deeds?

But even better than that, those finger-pointers may "see your good deeds and glorify God on the day he visits us."

There is no victory so sweet as that which comes through stead-fast surrender to the God who watches us all.

Dear God, help me not be bothered by watchful eyes but to value the opportunity to shine a light on You. Amen. —ML

What Do You Owe?

Give to everyone what you owe them: If you owe taxes, pay taxes; if revenue, then revenue; if respect, then respect; if honor, then honor.
ROMANS 13:7

There are few things that draw a nation together like the universal loathing of taxes. Whether you hate the paperwork or the principles, we can all agree that no one is that excited when tax day approaches.

But Paul sets up a parallel we can't ignore. Respect is to paying taxes as honor is to paying revenue.

When we think something has value, when we find a worthy product and want it for our own, we pay revenue. We honor the manufacturer of that product through monetary compensation.

And when we respect the government that enforces our laws, fixes our roads, and generally keeps our country a civil place to live, we pay taxes.

Taxes are not a punishment. Taxes are an opportunity to pay respect where it is due. And if you don't think it is due, just try living for any extended period of time in another country—preferably a developing nation. You'll soon develop oodles of respect for your home government.

The system might be cumbersome and imperfect, but the exercise is a useful one. It's a reminder to be in submission to one another. We don't pay taxes merely for our personal benefit, we pay taxes to create benefits for our neighbor too.

Dear God our King, help me to be grateful for the system of government that allows me the freedom to worship You without fear. Amen. —ML

Whatevers

Finally, brothers and sisters, whatever is true,
whatever is noble, whatever is right, whatever is pure,
whatever is lovely, whatever is admirable—if anything is
excellent or praiseworthy—think about such things.
PHILIPPIANS 4:8

For some time now it's been trendy for younger people to use the term *whatever* as a way of expressing either derision (with emphasis on the second syllable, snarky tone fully employed: what-EV-er) or a laid-back approach (often accompanied by a shrug of the shoulder and shortened to *whatevs*).

Either of those usages would seem rather inappropriate in our verse here. The *whatevers* that Paul employs are used in the traditional sense, to mean "anything and everything." So we are to think on anything and everything that is true, noble, right, and so on.

Anything and everything? You can see the eye rolls now, can't you? It's the same expression you get when you tell children they only have two more pages of homework to do. "Two more pages? But that will take for-EV-er!"

Anything and everything? That will take a long time. And that's the point. Because if we are busy thinking of anything and everything that falls in this list of attributes, we won't have any time left to think about whatever is deceitful, low-down, wrong, impure, ugly, despicable—anything mediocre or unworthy.

Of course, you are thinking, *Can anyone really achieve this?* Maybe not. But won't it be lovely to try?

Dear Lord of all, thank You for always challenging me to
be a better me. Help me make You proud. Amen. —ML

All Things

I can do all things through him who strengthens me.
PHILIPPIANS 4:13 NRSV

There may be no other verse in the Bible whose meaning is stretched farther than that of Philippians 4:13. "I can do all things" has become a Christian slogan of sorts—meant to convey the idea that literally anything is possible through Christ. And not just that anything is possible, but we can do it!

But this verse doesn't say that *anything* is possible. Rather, this verse reveals the secret Paul tells us he has learned—"the secret of being well-fed and of going hungry, of having plenty and of being in need" (verse 12). The secret is that Christ gives Paul strength so that he can find contentment, no matter what the circumstance. Christ supplies what he lacks.

So what's the issue with the Christian-slogan version of this verse? The problem is that it often sets up people to focus more on what they can *do* rather than on what God *supplies*. And a further problem is, when the person fails at a thing, gets tired, or—heaven forbid—complains, there is a tendency among Christians to judge that person as somehow not relying on God's strength enough, not believing enough, or not trying hard enough. And that is simply wrong and not at all what Paul intended.

Dear Jesus, thank You for giving us strength to endure any situation. Thank You for supplying what we need so we don't ever have to worry. Amen. —ML

With Feeling

*"How often I have longed to gather your children
together, as a hen gathers her chicks under
her wings, and you were not willing."*
MATTHEW 23:37

There are some verses of the Bible that are beautiful because of what the words say, and there are some that are beautiful because of what they show. This verse is probably a little of both.

Where in the world did we ever get this greeting-card image of Jesus as a soft, flowy sort of person, with a mild expression and a gentle attitude? Certainly He could be gentle, but this was not His only disposition.

Jesus was fully human. And as such, He had the full range of human emotions. We witness some of that here in Matthew 23. He begins the chapter slightly irritated and a little bit sarcastic. Then as we move into the seven woes, we feel His wrath. Jesus is not just unhappy with these Pharisees—He is righteously enraged.

But Jesus never loses it. And beneath the anger is a current of sorrow and compassion. This comes out as He speaks to the city of Jerusalem, like a father who is disappointed for his child—not so much because the child is a disappointment (though that may well be true) but because the child's future will be less than what it should be.

Emotions, strong feelings—these are not un-Christian as a rule. We should feel strongly about things that matter. But we need to spend some time figuring out what really does matter.

Lord, help us to speak in meaningful ways. Amen. —ML

The Problem with the World

Do not love the world or anything in the world. If anyone loves the world, love for the Father is not in them. For everything in the world— the lust of the flesh, the lust of the eyes, and the pride of life— comes not from the Father but from the world.
1 JOHN 2:15–16

Women tend to not discuss lust in reference to themselves. It's far easier to talk about the problem men have with lust. But the problem is there among females all the same.

Our world is filled with visuals that entice us to want what we should not have. Sexual depictions of men and women flash on our screens, even in the margins of otherwise relatively respectable websites. Images of gorgeous fattening desserts beg us to eat them and not be sorry. Romantic stories of adultery fool us into rooting for the breakup of marriages. Tempting images of luxurious clothing deceive us into thinking we deserve to splurge.

With all of these different flavors of temptation, and given that women are often the ones doing the shopping and purchasing, it seems women are highly likely to fall into some kind of lust any day of the week—perhaps even more so than their male counterparts!

Sisters in Christ, we cannot pretend that these images, stories, and sounds have no effect on us. We have to start with an honest confession of where we are weak. Then we can lean on one another for support and prayer.

Dear God, help me to be open to being held accountable. Amen. —ML

Don't Bite

*If you bite and devour each other, watch out
or you will be destroyed by each other.*
GALATIANS 5:15

In every nursery in the world, there are children known as "biters." The designation requires no explanation. Some kids bite as a way of expressing anger or frustration, and some kids just bite for no apparent reason.

In every community in the world, there are women who could be labeled this way as well. They criticize sharply, with no compassion. They offer up insults instead of encouragement. Of course, it's not only females who do this. But women are particularly good at verbal weaponry.

So what should you do when you encounter a "biter"? First, try not to bite back. You can try to engage the person in friendly conversation, but if she is set on a path of destruction, this may not work in the moment.

Sometimes the best course of action is just to walk away. Then show kindness to the woman at a separate time. Try to understand her. There's almost always a reason people lash out in this way (with the exception of those preschool biters).

Finally, be mindful of your own words. Perhaps you are not the kind to shout at someone in a group, but do you say spiteful things about a person or ridicule her in private? This is just as destructive as the public display, perhaps more so.

Instead, focus on the Fruit of the Spirit noted farther along in this chapter: love, joy, peace, patience, kindness, goodness, gentleness, faithfulness, and self-control (see verses 22, 23).

Lord, help my words to heal and not hurt. Amen. —ML

Abigail

She was an intelligent and beautiful woman.
1 SAMUEL 25:3

Abigail is a beautiful example of what happens to a woman when she listens to God and puts wisdom into practice.

When her foolish husband, Nabal, denied David and his men any provisions, Abigail acted quickly to repair the damage. She assessed the situation and realized immediately what must be done. She bravely went against her husband's wishes and took supplies in secret to David. In doing so, she saved at least two men from ruin: her surly husband, who would have been killed by David otherwise, and David, who would have had unnecessary bloodshed on his hands.

Though Abigail did act against her husband's wishes, she did not do so lightly. She was not just looking out for herself. Her husband was a very wealthy and wicked man. He had a whole household of servants depending on him. If she had not done what she did, every man in the place would have been killed.

Abigail's speech to David was another example of brilliance. She belittled Nabal right off the bat and told David it was God who was keeping David from bloodshed. She balanced her own humility with praise of his greatness, carefully weaving a picture of him as one blessed by the Lord, and even alluding to David's past exploits ("the lives of your enemies he [God] will hurl away as from the pocket of a sling," verse 29). Every word was well chosen.

And in the end, her wisdom won the day—saving the lives of her household and eventually securing her a place in David's palace.

Lord God, help me be a discerning woman. Amen. —ML

Approaching the Throne

"And if I perish, I perish."
ESTHER 4:16

Terrified. Heart beating into throat, sweat beading on forehead and upper lip, tears threatening to fall out of the pools developing in her eyes. She must have been utterly and completely frozen with fear.

Have you ever felt this kind of fear? The kind that comes from taking on a task that seems much too large for you, where many people are depending on you? The kind of fear that comes from doing something you've never done before?

Esther dressed in her finest robes and walked, step after agonizing step, down the hallway toward the inner court of the palace. She paused before stepping in front of the king's hall. In a moment, he would see her. And either death would come, or she would be accepted.

Aren't you glad that when we approach the throne of our King, we can do so with confidence, knowing we will receive mercy and grace (see Hebrews 4:16)? How great a blessing it is to be able to go to our Lord and King at any time with our troubles, never fearing His rejection!

Esther could have run away—she could have let her doubts take over. But she remembered who she was—Hadassah, the Jew, the queen. And she knew that all the Jews in Susa were praying for her. Depending on her.

And she took that last step.

Who is depending on us to step out in faith?

*Dear God, thank You for always allowing us into
Your presence, anytime. Amen. —ML*

Grief-Worn

*Heal me, LORD, for my bones are in agony. My soul
is in deep anguish. How long, LORD, how long?*
PSALM 6:2–3

Like a flooded river, pushing past its banks and uprooting trees.
Like a gray drizzle of rain that never stops. Like an old elephant
sitting on one's chest. Like a cliff, eroded by the wind and crumbling.
Like a night with no stars.

We struggle to find ways of expressing the bone-crushing weariness of grief. Sometimes it feels that if we could just put it into
words, maybe we could get past the sorrow.

But the psalmist has given us words: "I am worn out from my
groaning. All night long I flood my bed with weeping and drench
my couch with tears. My eyes grow weak with sorrow; they fail
because of all my foes" (verses 6–7).

It is somehow comforting to know that souls from thousands of
years ago can speak to us about the same feelings we have today.
And that even though there is still pain and trouble and sorrow,
there is also still our Lord God, who never changes: "The LORD
has heard my weeping. The LORD has heard my cry for mercy; the
LORD accepts my prayer" (verses 8–9).

*Dear God, hear me when I am sad and feel alone. Show me You
are with me and that my grief will not go on forever. Amen. —ML*

True Life

Command them to do good, to be rich in good deeds, and to be generous and willing to share. In this way they will lay up treasure for themselves as a firm foundation for the coming age, so that they may take hold of the life that is truly life.
1 TIMOTHY 6:18–19

Have you ever watched one of those hoarding shows on TV? They are often heartbreaking. People store up material goods in an effort to fill some hole in their lives, or as an extreme way of making sure they never go without.

Though Paul wasn't talking about hoarders in his letter to Timothy, he was referring to people who operate on a similar principle. These rich people "put their hope in wealth, which is so uncertain" (verse 17). They surround themselves with a life that has a certain look to it, a certain theme, a certain brand name.

What is the life that is truly life to you? What does it look like? What does it feel like? Where are you when you have it? Is it catalog worthy, a picture-perfect living room, with two-and-a-half kids and a dog? Or is it something dirtier, grittier, less pretty? Is it filled with people in need, or is it filled with people in power?

Whatever it looks like, I'm sure it doesn't include piles and piles of garbage lining the walls. No true life can be found there.

Dear Provider of everything we need and everything we enjoy, help me to let go of stuff and to take hold of life. Amen. —ML

It's a Drag

For God cannot be tempted by evil, nor does he tempt anyone; but each person is tempted when they are dragged away by their own evil desire and enticed.
JAMES 1:13–14

The black-raspberry chocolate-chip ice cream called. You didn't mean to buy it. You were just minding your own business, buying groceries—healthy food, like fruit, vegetables, and whole wheat things. But it called you over to the freezer aisle. And somehow you left the store with it. After that, everything's a blur. But now there's an empty pint-size ice cream container in the trash can. And you feel perhaps a little sick.

It's a strong image—being "dragged away" by evil desire. Not that wanting ice cream is necessarily evil, but surely we have all felt the pull of desire before. Whether it was greed, pride, lust, or rage, we've felt the tide rising up in us and we've known the tug of the current on our core. If we've not prepared for this moment, we will lose the fight. Sometimes we're so swept away that we don't even know we are supposed to fight.

So how can we prepare for these times? "Let perseverance finish its work so that you may be mature and complete, not lacking anything. If any of you lacks wisdom, you should ask God, who gives generously to all without finding fault, and it will be given to you" (verses 4–5).

Dear Lord, forgive me for blaming You when I fail. Help me to be complete so I can fight against my desires. Amen. —ML

Wash and Go

*"I thought that he would surely. . .stand and
call on the name of the LORD his God."*
2 KINGS 5:11

Pop Quiz: When was the last time you asked God for something
and had no idea how it could possibly occur? When was the last
time you asked God for something, and you already had a pretty
good idea of how you would like it to occur?

We often make plans first and then ask God to bless them.
Naaman, the army commander for Aram, had a good idea how his
leprosy could be cured. It involved symbolic gestures and perhaps
an appearance by God himself. But Elisha, God's prophet, told
him to just go wash in the river seven times. Simple. Too simple
for an army commander.

Maybe you have a plan about who you will marry, where you
will live, or what career you will have. If you are also a follower of
God, you should ask Him for guidance. Now here's where things
get tricky. If we ask God what to do to achieve a goal, He might
just answer us. *But that's what I want,* you think.

Is it?

Are you ready to accept God's instructions, even if they seem
silly—or extra hard? What if they involve embarrassment? What if
you have to apologize, or forgive someone who doesn't deserve it?
What if they involve a true leap of faith? What if His instructions
mean waiting. . .a long time? Will you follow His guidance then?

Dear God, help me to obey You, no matter what. Amen. —ML

Not Lost for Words

"The Holy Spirit will teach you at that time what you should say."
LUKE 12:12

Many people feel, um, uh, awkward about talking to others about, uh, well, er, you know. . .this Jesus thing. For some it's just an overall problem with introversion, for others it's a problem of knowing the right thing to say. What if we mess up? What if we get the details wrong? What if they ask a question we don't know how to answer?

We don't usually have this anxiety about other types of church outreach projects—we can pass out water bottles, balloons, or snack bags with never a nervous twitch. And most of us don't have this problem with other conversations. While at the park, we can talk to strangers about dogs. Or we can talk about last night's episode of *American Pop Talent Dancer Idol* with anyone who'll listen.

But the Jesus thing. That's a problem. Jesus tries to calm fears about this when He's talking with His disciples. Whenever they have to defend themselves and their beliefs, they don't have to worry about their words—the Holy Spirit will come to the rescue.

And if you think about it, if we are not so worried about how God will provide and care for our neighbors and ourselves in other ways, why should we worry about how He will provide for us in this way? Surely the God who spoke the world into existence with His words can help us figure out how to talk about His Son. Right?

God, help us trust You more. Amen. —ML

Save an Hour Today

"Can any one of you by worrying add a single hour to your life?"
MATTHEW 6:27

Jesus has a sense of humor. If you don't know this, go and read the Gospels some more. Sometimes the funniest bits of His speeches come from the comparisons He makes.

In this rhetorical question from Matthew 6, you can hear a note of sarcasm in Jesus' voice. Because, of course, worrying does add up in hours—hours of waste and anxiety, hours of stress and arguments, hours and hours and hours of headaches. But none of that is life. It's somewhere on the path to death.

This whole passage is humorous, if you think about what it might have sounded like on the first run. The image of birds working in the fields and putting up crops in the barns, or of King Solomon dressed like a flower—these would have had the crowd smiling, for sure. And you can almost hear the rousing cheer go up at the end: "Do not worry about tomorrow. . . . Each day has enough trouble of its own" (verse 34). Preach it, Jesus!

This is often what Jesus did—He didn't just say words, He used His words to create change. It's what He did with the moneylenders in the temple and with the woman caught in adultery. And it's what He's doing here—using a little comic relief to lighten the burdens of a bunch of worrywarts. So smile. Don't worry. Be joyful.

Dear Giver of all good things, please help us to turn from worry and grow in trust. Amen. —ML

It Keeps You Young

*Sarah was past the age of childbearing. So Sarah
laughed to herself as she thought, "After I am worn out
and my lord is old, will I now have this pleasure?"*
GENESIS 18:11–12

Almost any older woman today who received this news would not
be laughing. At least, not in a happy way. Maybe in a nervous,
gotta-laugh-or-else-I'll-cry kind of way.

Sarah's husband, Abraham, had seen a century go by. And she
herself was not far behind. Yes, if this kind of thing had happened
in today's world, you better believe that woman would be marching
into her gyno's office and demanding some answers.

But this child brought joy to Sarah's life. "God has brought me
laughter," Sarah said at the birth of her son, "and everyone who
hears about this will laugh with me" (Genesis 21:6). Abraham even
gave the boy a name that means "he laughs": Isaac.

And Sarah went on to live close to forty more years after the
boy's birth. The boy seemed to be a fountain of youth for his
mother. Surely the day of his birth was not the last day he brought
her laughter. Children are like that. They can be little bundles of
joy that keep spreading smiles even into their teenage years. Of
course, they can bring a lot of tears too. But somehow the laughter
seems to balance it all out.

Laughter, in whatever form, is a beautiful, powerful thing. It
can take our minds off some of the hardest parts of life. It can form
connections between people. It can sow seeds of peace.

And it's wonderful to have a God who laughs with us, even at
His own jokes—like ninety-year-old new mothers.

Dear God, help me laugh more. Amen. —ML

Patterns of Redemption

"If anyone sins and does what is forbidden in any of the LORD's commands, even though they do not know it, they are guilty and will be held responsible."
LEVITICUS 5:17

Leviticus does not rank high on the favorite books of the Bible list for most people. It is a book filled with detailed regulations and instructions. To be fair, any book that has a section in it entitled "Regulations about Defiling Molds" is not likely to make it on most people's bedside reading stacks.

But there is something very beautiful and comforting about Leviticus. And it's found in its patterns. Over and over again, the Lord gives to Moses paths of atonement for His people. He covers almost every area of sin—even the area of unknowing sin. And for every kind of sin, He either offers a way out, or is giving a warning that people would be extremely foolish not to heed.

Over and over, God is providing a way to restore Israel's position before Him. He wants everyone to be included, so He offers multiple ways to make offerings—for those who are wealthy and for the poorest among them. Over and over again, He shows that He knows us intimately—He knows what evil we will get ourselves into, He knows every detail of our daily lives. And over and over again, He reveals that He wants us, even in our mess.

Thank You, Lord, for loving us so consistently. Amen. —ML

Bringing Down the House

The wise woman builds her house, but with her
own hands the foolish one tears hers down.
PROVERBS 14:1

Have you ever watched a bird building its nest? Each piece is selected carefully. If the material is too big and bulky, it might cause a hole in the nest or a weak spot. If something is too bright, it might attract the wrong kind of attention. The best pieces are those that fit and blend right in—they are strong and supportive, but in the end you don't even see them.

The materials to build a family are not all that varied. It takes love, patience, and wisdom. No household will survive long (at least, not in any healthy sense) without love. From love comes forgiveness and understanding. Love is the sticky glue that holds everyone together.

People change and grow. Patience allows a household to be flexible—giving everyone space to breathe and reach up and out.

Wisdom provides the structure for family life. Wisdom sets out rules and goals, creating a solid framework within which people can grow and learn and create and be challenged.

A wise woman works constantly at weaving these pieces together into a strong body. The foolish woman is inconstant. She cannot ever settle on a plan, so she keeps tearing things down and starting over. And in all her busyness, she forgets to love, and she loses patience.

The wise woman keeps building, long after the "eggs" hatch.

Dear Father, help us to be wise builders. Amen. —ML

Don't Look Now

A heart at peace gives life to the body, but envy rots the bones.
PROVERBS 14:30

The rise of online social networks has created a lot of benefits. Friends who are spread across the world can reconnect. Grandparents can feel more involved in their grandchildren's lives. People can reach out to one another quickly and conveniently.

When people post about themselves online, they often choose the highlights—the most positive parts of the week, month, or year. Sunny vacation pictures in which everyone is smiling. Photos of new cars and graduations.

So when we look at the "profiles" of the people we know, we miss the full picture. And sometimes, this tricks us into believing that their lives must be better than ours. Their jobs are more fulfilling, their families get along better, their cars are newer, their skin is smoother, and on top of all that, they have better shoes.

Now some of that might even be true, but not all of it. Yet if you expose yourself over and over to these best snippets of people's lives, you are bound to start feeling a little unsatisfied with your own. A little irritated. And a little (or a lot) envious.

So what's the solution? Well, you could stop looking so much. But also, take a reality check. Look at what you revealed this week, month, or year. Then remember a bit of the struggle that went on behind those shiny smiles and happy sound bites. Your "friends" are no different.

Dear God, help me not compare
my life to others' lives. Amen. —ML

The Answer Is No One

The LORD is my light and my salvation—whom shall I fear?
PSALM 27:1

Fear. It can stop you in your tracks. It can grab you by the throat and suffocate the words right out of you. It can keep you from being the person God created you to be.

Many of us have legitimate reasons to be afraid. Maybe there are people in our lives who threaten us. Maybe we've been through traumatic experiences. Maybe because of illness or poor health choices or both, our lives are more fragile.

But living in fear is not living fully. And God wants us to have a full life.

"The LORD is my light and my salvation." When you accept Christ as your Savior, you get certain things in return. You get an understanding of good and evil—and you get the knowledge that you are on the side of good. You get a clearer vision of the darkness in your life—and you get a Friend who is always with you, no matter how dark things seem to be. And you get peace—through knowing your place before God. That you stand in His grace, blameless and pure, and you have a place in heaven created just for you. A place no one can take away.

So be as careful as you need to be. Be smart and alert. Spend time and get help to heal and become strong. But don't let whatever has happened to you or whoever has done something to you stop you from becoming all that God created you to be.

Dear Jesus, help me to feel You at my side. Amen. —ML

Perfect

*"My grace is sufficient for you, for my
power is made perfect in weakness."*
2 CORINTHIANS 12:9

Perfectionism has problems. In fact, the constant striving for perfection can sometimes cause people to be unsatisfied, critical, ungrateful, and impossible to live with.

Yet it's good to want to be the best, right? Sure, it's good to want that. But it's not so good to think that you can achieve it all by yourself.

God turns human perfectionism on its head. He says, "I don't want you to be perfect. I'm going to make you perfect. What I need you to be is pliable." He needs us to bend—to His will, to His way, to His heart. And to bend, we can't be perfect pieces of straight, rock-hard wood. We've got to allow a little weakness.

It's time to celebrate imperfection. Like Paul, we need to "boast all the more gladly about [our] weaknesses, so that Christ's power may rest on" us (verse 9). We can take delight in "weaknesses, in insults, in hardships, in persecutions, in difficulties" (verse 10). Then, like Paul, we can say, "When I am weak, then I am strong" (verse 10). How is that for a paradox?

Instead of working so hard to get everything right, let God do His work in you. Instead of expecting so much from yourself, let your hope rest in God. Instead of commiserating that you are weak, glory in God's strength working through you. Instead of desiring perfection, desire to please Him.

*Dear God, please forgive me for my mistakes. Please help
me to let Your power be strong in me. Amen.* —ML

Quit Fooling Yourself

Nothing in all creation is hidden from God's sight.
HEBREWS 4:13

We are funny creatures. And as followers of God, we are hilarious.

What a ragtag parade of people God has in His crew! Criminals and saints, fools and sages, champions and failures.

And you can count on it that every single one of us at one time or another has thought we could slip something past Him.

It started with Adam and Eve. That image of them trying to hide from God in the garden has always seemed the silliest part of their story. As if some camouflage could keep them from the Creator of every leaf, bush, and tree! If not for the seriousness of the situation, God would have certainly laughed at their folly.

But the silliness doesn't end there. Cain tried to plead ignorance. David set up an elaborate ruse to hide adultery. Judas kissed Jesus, greeting Him as if a whole detachment of soldiers and accusers were not standing behind him.

Ridiculous, aren't we? Who do we think we are? Who do we think God is?

It's time to put an end to these shenanigans. It's time to come clean. If you've been sinning and trying to hide it—face it. God knows. It's time to fess up and take the consequences. "Everything is uncovered and laid bare before the eyes of him to whom we must give account" (Hebrews 4:13).

Don't be another ridiculous character in the story of the world. It's not really that funny.

God, I need to be honest about _____.
Forgive me. Amen. —ML

Temporary

*Our light and momentary troubles are achieving
for us an eternal glory that far outweighs them all.*
2 CORINTHIANS 4:17

Everyone gets tired sometimes. It does not matter what kind of life you lead, where you live, or what level of hardship you endure. Even people living in the lap of luxury get weary of their lives.

No matter what conditions you are experiencing, it's important to remember that they are temporary. Is your current schedule stressing you out? It's temporary. Is a medical condition making life a daily struggle? It's temporary. Is a family argument weighing you down? It's temporary.

Temporary. Not just because someday we'll all go to heaven and all will be well. But because every minute of our lives has the potential for change.

Sometimes all it takes is a left turn instead of a right. A new path. A new thought. A different chapter. A surprise. A joke. A visit.

What's wonderful is we don't have to just wait for that change to come to us. We can be that change for someone else. We can go to someone who is suffering and struggling, and give her something new to think about. Even if just for a moment.

"We fix our eyes not on what is seen, but on what is unseen, since what is seen is temporary, but what is unseen is eternal" (verse 18). It's a good verse to put up on your mirror. Today is temporary. You can have hope in tomorrow.

*Dear Lord, help me to be focused on the
eternal— not the temporary. Amen. —ML*

Whatever You Ask

"If you believe, you will receive whatever you ask for in prayer."
MATTHEW 21:22

The sky's the limit. That's essentially what Jesus told His disciples here. He said you can make a fig tree wither with a word, or have a mountain throw itself into the sea. Magical things. The stuff of fairy tales. Wild stuff can happen through prayer.

Do you really believe that? In truth, probably nobody you know really wants to wither a tree or throw a mountain anywhere. But what about healing a friend and getting rid of cancer? What about making the war, whatever war is going on right now, stop? What about just paying rent?

Do you really believe that you will receive whatever you ask?

Think about that for a minute. Or three.

Let's change the question a little. Do you really believe? Will you receive whatever you ask? Think about that for another minute. Or four.

Christians have nice answers for these questions when younger Christians ask them. We say that God works through our prayers; that if we are in God's will, that we will ask for things that God wants to happen anyway. That if we don't have the right motives, we won't get what we ask.

And those things are all most likely true. But this illustration Jesus made here to His disciples has a different flavor to it, doesn't it? Here, He seems to be pushing us to want something more. Something we think is impossible.

So what is your mountain?

God, help me truly believe. Amen. —ML

Acceptance

Believers in our glorious Lord Jesus Christ must not show favoritism.
JAMES 2:1

James is a great one for speaking plainly. In his words on favoritism, he painfully points out how his listeners were treating the poor badly and showing undue favor to the rich.

But were James writing to your church today, who would be the subjects of his discussion? To whom do you show less kindness, care, love, or generosity than you show others? Who do you offer more respect, honor, or favors simply because of who they are, what they do, or what they have?

Let's just consider some categories, shall we? Who do you look down on? Fat people. People who use food stamps. Divorced people. People with mental illness. Walmart shoppers. White people. Tattooed people. Non-tattooed people. Smokers. Alcoholics. Old people. Black people. Vegans. Fast-food eaters. Ex-convicts. Children. Loud, obnoxious people. Lawyers. Democrats. Republicans. Adulterers. Homeschoolers. Celebrities. Hispanic people. Wealthy people. Refugees. Quiet people. Bosses. Employees. Waiters. Customer service people. IRS agents. Homeless people.

Did you flinch at any of those? Is there one (or more) of those groups who would give you the heebie-jeebies if they sat down next to you in church? Is there one (or more) of those groups you would treat better than others?

It seems likely that very few of us are completely free from some hint of prejudice against some group of people. Be honest about that today.

God, help me to love others as You love me. Amen. —ML

Covered

*The waters swelled so mightily. . .that all the high
mountains under the whole heaven were covered.*
GENESIS 7:19 NRSV

Noah's ark. All those cute and colorful animals in a big boat make
for a page-turner in kid country. But this is not a child-friendly story.
All the other animals died a horrible drowning death. And so did
all the people not on the ark.

It's a sad story. A story of a heartbroken God and a heartless
world. It's a story of deep sorrow, as deep as the floodwaters.

It's striking to think about this amount of water. Enough to flood
not only cities but whole countries, whole continents! Enough not
just to swallow up skyscrapers but to make mountains disappear.
Mountains. Think about that. The highest, most majestic, closest-
to-the-heavens places on earth—covered by dark, swirling seas.

Have your mountains ever been covered? Have you ever felt
so deeply sad that the highest and brightest points of your life
became invisible?

How do you swim to the top of an ocean of sorrow? How do
you find dry land?

"God remembered Noah" (Genesis 8:1 NRSV). God remembered
Noah, because before the first raindrops fell, long before the
sadness even set in, "Noah walked with God" (6:9 NRSV).

And God will remember you. If you walk with Him daily, when
the rains come, when sorrow floods your soul, when your mountains
crumble, He will remember you. And He will save you.

God, help me to hope in You, even when I'm sad. Amen. —ML

Only God Knows

The heart is deceitful above all things and
beyond cure. Who can understand it?
JEREMIAH 17:9

In the middle of a conversation Jeremiah was having with the Lord about sin and trust, and the general untrustworthiness of man, Jeremiah inserts this comment about the heart. "Who can understand it?"

How many times have you asked that question? Maybe it was about your own longings, or those of a friend. Maybe it was about your teenage daughter. Maybe it was about that guy you liked who fell for that super-snobby, awful girl. Maybe it was about someone's marriage breaking up. Or someone you looked up to, who let you down.

God is quick to answer Jeremiah's question. "I the LORD search the heart and examine the mind, to reward each person according to their conduct, according to what their deeds deserve" (verse 10).

Who understands our hearts? God does. He's the only one who can see inside us, see past our fronts and disguises, see through our actions, and know our hearts.

So if someone you love is puzzling you, or you find your own desires confusing, don't call your therapist. At least, ask God first.

Dear God, figuring out what I want and why I do the things
I do is sometimes tricky. Help me, please. Amen. —ML

One and Only

*This is how God showed his love among us: He sent his one
and only Son into the world that we might live through him.*
1 JOHN 4:9

If you are a mother, you know the fears that accompany the first
time you let your child out into the world on his or her own. And
if you aren't a mother, you can probably think of a time when you
had to be separated from someone, some place, or something
that meant the world to you.

Mothers who watch their children go into the mission field or
military service must receive an extra measure of guts from God.
To let a child go off to college is nothing compared to watching
a child leave for a country you cannot reach in less than several
hours, maybe to a place where you can have very limited contact
(if at all) for a long, long time.

It's not even the reality of these situations that is the hardest
thing to bear. It's the what-ifs—what a mother's imagination can
conjure up. And that is limitless!

God has one Son. And He let that one precious Child go into a
dangerous world. God didn't have to imagine what would happen.
He knew the horrible pain His Child would suffer and that He
would die. God the Father knew that, and He still let His Son go.

And God did that to show us His love.

Dear Father, let me live a life worthy of Your love. Amen. —ML

Made by God

For we are God's handiwork, created in Christ Jesus to do good works, which God prepared in advance for us to do.
EPHESIANS 2:10

Have you forgotten how marvelous you are?

Yes, I'm talking to you.

When was the last time you considered your wonderful body? When did you last stop and think about how amazing it is that your brain does all it does in a day? Have you listened to your own heart beating? Have you taken time to breathe—*really* breathe?

When was the last time you enjoyed fresh air? When did you last use all your senses to appreciate a moment? When did you last work hard at something? When did you last take pride in your work? Have you ever used all of your body to create something amazing? When have you used your abilities to serve someone else?

You are God's handiwork. You are handmade by God. If there were a manufacturer's label tattooed on your body, it would say MADE BY GOD.

And what were we made for? To do good works. Which good works? The ones God has designed for us especially to do. What are those? If you don't know, you better ask the manufacturer. And in the meantime, you might as well try the nearest good work that needs to be done in your neighborhood.

What have you got to lose? You are designed by the Creator of the world.

God, Your gifts amaze me. Help me
not to waste them. Amen. —ML

White

"Though your sins are like scarlet, they shall be as white as snow."
ISAIAH 1:18

Big, wet flakes. They fall softly, slowly, but weigh heavily on the branches of the unsuspecting trees. So heavy are they, the limbs creak and sway under the weight.

Everything turns white. Layer upon layer of the purest, brightest white. The world is no longer gray and brown and green and blue. White clouds, white sky, white trees, white yard, white fence, white roof.

Imagine if all the corners of your heart were changed to become as pure, bright, and clean as a fresh layer of snow.

It seems like it would take a lot of layers to blot out the dark red stain of sin, doesn't it? A lot of acts of repentance? A lot of apologies? A lot of prayers or hymns of worship?

In this chapter of Isaiah, however, God paints a different picture. He has had "more than enough" (verse 11) sacrifices and offerings. He "cannot bear" (verse 13) any more feasts or festivals or worship gatherings.

What does He want the people to do instead? "Stop doing wrong. Learn to do right; seek justice. Defend the oppressed. Take up the cause of the fatherless; plead the case of the widow" (verses 16–17).

He does not want words that mean nothing or promises that don't go anywhere. He does not need songs and parties and celebrations. He wants obedience.

Stop doing wrong. Learn to do right. Clean, bright, pure, and simple. Like snow.

Dear God, help me to obey You. Amen. —ML

Make the Most of It

Be very careful, then, how you live—not as unwise but as wise, making the most of every opportunity, because the days are evil.
EPHESIANS 5:15–16

In this fifth chapter of Paul's letter to the Ephesians, he writes about several things that are not proper behavior for God's holy people: everything from off-color jokes to drunkenness. Now if you aren't sold on the idea that these kinds of things lead to more serious evil-doing, Paul presents one more point to consider.

You don't have time.

If you are a believer, you just don't have time. There's too much to do in this world. You've got people to forgive, joy to share, good news to bring. You've got needs to be met, shoulders to be cried on, free hugs to offer, and desperate people to comfort. You've got neighbors to love and a great, big, huge God to serve.

And you've got a lot to learn.

There's just not time for telling stupid jokes that hurt people or spouting obscenities. Just think of the time it takes to do damage control! There's not time for sexual immorality or for the hunting, gathering, and hoarding motivated by greed. There's not time for empty words—there's too much significant stuff that needs to be said. There's not time to get toasted—you need to have all your wits about you.

Wake up, slacker! Okay, Paul says "sleeper" (verse 14), but the meaning is clear. You've got work to do!

God, help me to make the most of every day I live. Amen. —ML

The Real Struggle

*Put on the full armor of God, so that you can
take your stand against the devil's schemes.*
EPHESIANS 6:11

One of the devil's best tools of destruction is distraction.

He distracts us from our goals. He makes the newspaper, a TV show, shopping online, or any other trivial thing seem so much more attractive than getting our to-do list done for the day. Sometimes he stretches this kind of minute-by-minute distraction into years of career-derailing wastefulness.

He distracts us from our people. He makes doing seem more important than loving, so we cook, clean, work, and earn but miss out on the detailed work of developing a relationship.

He distracts us from our true battleground. He makes it seem better to argue with friends, nag spouses, lash out at solicitors, or be enraged by government leaders than to fight a spiritual battle. "For our struggle is not against flesh and blood" (verse 12).

We should have those words memorized. When we get cut off in traffic—"our struggle is not against flesh and blood." When we get ridiculed by colleagues—"our struggle is not against flesh and blood." When we get hurt by those we love—"our struggle is not against flesh and blood."

And even when we are dissatisfied with our own bodies, the "struggle is not against flesh and blood." The real work to gain back our focus and defeat the devil's schemes of distraction begins with truth, righteousness, Gospel readiness, faith, salvation, the Word of God, and prayer.

*Dear mighty God, help me be fit for
the real battle at hand. Amen.—ML*

Sarah's Daughters

This is the way the holy women of the past who
put their hope in God used to adorn themselves.
1 PETER 3:5

Some of us have looked at 1 Peter 3 and belittled the author's image of beautiful women as quiet, weak, mousey beings living in the shadow of their husbands. Not exactly an attractive interpretation, nor is it fair.

Look again at Peter's letter. "Wives, in the same way. . . " (verse 1). What way? Flip back to chapter 2, verse 21. In the same way as the steps of Jesus Christ. Oh, that way.

So, "in the same way," do what? "Submit yourselves to your own husbands, so that. . .they may be won over without words by the behavior of their wives, when they see the purity and reverence of your lives" (verses 1–2). Purity and reverence require an incredible amount of self-control and self-respect. Such women don't even have to speak—everyone knows what kind of people they are by the way they live.

"Your beauty. . .should be that of your inner self" (verses 3–4). Who wouldn't want a man to value her inner beauty rather than her face or clothes or hair?

Peter then tells us this is the way the holy women of the past lived—holy women like Sarah, "who obeyed Abraham" (verse 6). Don't get stuck there. Keep moving: "You are her daughters if you do what is right and do not give way to fear" (verse 6).

Sarah's daughters are strong and courageous, beautiful inside and out.

Now who wants to be a daughter of Sarah?

God, help me to be strong and pure and
worthy of Your praise. Amen. —ML

Say It Slow

*Everyone should be quick to listen, slow to
speak and slow to become angry.*
JAMES 1:19

Slow to speak. Slow to speak. Slow to speak. The words of James make us slow down just to say them correctly.

There's a myth that has had great influence for some time now. It goes something like this: To speak your mind means speaking the first thing that comes to your head. And to be authentic, you should always say what is on your mind.

But it is a mistake to equate authenticity with immediacy. How often is it that the first thoughts that flit through your head in response to anything are words of truth—words that fully and accurately represent your opinion or understanding of a subject? Now, let that "anything" be part of an argument, in particular, an argument where someone is accusing you of something, voicing her opposition to what you are doing, or even attacking your character. Now how often are the first words that race through your ruffled-up mind representative of the truth? How often are they kind? How often are they worth saying? How often would they be capable of producing righteousness?

For that is the goal spoken of here. James's message continues in verses 20 and 21: "because human anger does not produce the righteousness that God desires. Therefore, get rid of all moral filth and the evil that is so prevalent and humbly accept the word planted in you, which can save you."

Speed kills. Slow down.

Dear God, help me to bite my tongue more often. Amen. —ML

Enforced Gratitude

They were also to stand every morning to thank and praise the Lord.
1 Chronicles 23:30

Ugly, ill-fitting, handmade sweaters. Hand-me-down clothes from two decades and two sizes ago. Landscaping tools when you live in an apartment building. A puzzle that is missing two pieces.

There are just some gifts for which it is hard to be thankful. And there are just some days when gratitude does not come easily. Don't you wish you could appoint someone to be thankful on your behalf?

The Israelites had the Levites. David appointed them to help Aaron's descendants with the service of the temple of the Lord. One of their jobs was to "stand every morning to thank and praise the Lord." They did this in the evening as well.

They also had thank offerings. It seems it would be far easier at times to offer a thank offering to burn—would handmade sweaters work?—than to actually say words of thanks, and far, far simpler than actually feeling thankful.

But for every awkward gift we receive or uncomfortable moment in life we endure, there must be at least a hundred good things our Father gives us that we can and should feel thankful for.

So try this. Appoint yourself to be your own Levite. Get up and stand every morning and thank and praise the Lord (try the short prayer below). Do it at night before you climb into bed as well.

After a while, you may even find yourself wearing an ugly sweater.

Dear Lord, I give thanks to You, for You are good,
and Your love endures forever. Amen. —ML

Planting

*"I planted the seed, Apollos watered it,
but God has been making it grow."*
1 CORINTHIANS 3:6

Apparently there were "Team Paul" and "Team Apollos" factions forming among the Corinthians. Paul puts a stop to this by pointing out that "neither the one who plants nor the one who waters is anything, but only God, who makes things grow" (verse 7).

Now some might bristle at this. Perhaps they want more acclaim for planting Gospel seeds. But it is a great comfort to know that the work of salvation is not solely up to us. We are, as Paul says, "co-workers in God's service" (verse 9). It's very freeing to know and trust that we can simply ask a good question, strike up an interesting conversation with someone, or listen to a person's struggle with faith in Jesus, and by doing so, plant a seed in her that God can then grow.

Have you ever hesitated to engage in a spiritual discussion with a person because you didn't know how he would take it or you felt like you didn't have the time required to build a relationship with him?

Of course, in an ideal world we'd have time to sit and chat with everyone for days, and the coffee would be free. But the fact that our world isn't ideal should not prevent us from planting a seed. You just never know what might happen to it. And that makes for some exciting gardening.

*Dear God, thank You for allowing me to work for Your
kingdom. Help me to plant more seeds. Amen.* —ML

Disconnected

They have lost connection with the head, from whom the whole body, supported and held together by its ligaments and sinews, grows as God causes it to grow.
COLOSSIANS 2:19

Some people consider themselves deeply spiritual. They could go on for hours about mystical experiences. Other people think there is a certain proper spiritual component to everything we do—what we eat and drink, the clothes we wear, the books we read, etc.—and they want to tell you all about it and how you are not doing things the right way.

Now this isn't to say that people don't have spiritual experiences or that there are not spiritual components to many things we do. But anytime our own experience of God or our rules about how we get to God become the focus of our conversations, it's a red flag.

Why? Because what is important is knowing God Himself, through His Word, not knowing other people's visions of Him or a certain diet plan to be closer to Him. There is a risk in either getting too swept up in spiritual feelings about God or too stuck in practical plans for godly living. And the risk is that we miss Him altogether.

Paul reminds us that we are not just a heart or a bundle of emotions and swirling thoughts, nor are we a human rule book. We have to keep our heads, both our physical heads and the Head of our faith, because it is through the head that the whole body grows.

Dear God, help me to keep my head at all times. Amen. —ML

A Shadow

The law is only a shadow of the good things that are coming—not the realities themselves.
HEBREWS 10:1

Shadows are fun to play with. It's especially delightful to watch a child playing with shadows for the first time. He jumps on them and chases them, thinking he can catch a real person if he can catch a shadow. When the light is right, you may see small children standing in such a way so that their shadow can be the same "height" as that of their parents. "Look, I'm as big as you!"

But shadows are imperfect representations of actual people. Sometimes a person might be recognizable by the outline of his shadow, but when the shadow is stretched or compressed, it's hard to say if you are looking at a person, a tree, or a funny bush. Shadows show no features, no colors. They don't speak. They just point to the fact that there is a mass there, and behind the mass is the light.

So it is with the things we see and do on earth. The ways we live, move, grow, and worship are all just shadows of what God has in store for us. So if you are unhappy here—good news. These are just shadows. And if you are happy here—good news. These are just shadows. And if you are wondering if there's anything more than what's here—good news. These are just shadows. So somewhere there is a Light.

Dear God, help me not to spend time chasing shadows but looking to the Light. Amen. —ML

Earning Respect

"What have I done to deserve such kindness?"
RUTH 2:10 NLT

Have you ever been an outsider? Maybe you moved to a new neighborhood, switched jobs, or just started attending a new Bible study group. Maybe you moved to a whole new country. The beginning of any such transition can be uncomfortable.

Ruth gives an example of how to handle such transitions well. Find something to do. Do it well. Don't ask for any special favors. Let your work speak for you.

Ruth was in a disadvantageous position. She was from Moab, and the Israelites did not look favorably on the Moabites. She came to live in a strange land—the homeland of her mother-in-law, who didn't really want her to come in the first place. And the Israelites had experienced a great famine in the not-too-distant past, so they would still be dealing with the shadow of scarcity.

But she found a literal corner of a field to work in, and she worked hard. And this work caught the eye of someone in a very advantageous position. And that was where Ruth's story took a turn for the better.

For Ruth, this upswing didn't take that long. You might have to work longer or harder. You might wait years before feeling accepted as part of a new community. And you might have to do things you feel are beneath you, or are difficult or boring, or simply not what you had in mind. But all the while you are an outsider, decide to be the best outsider you can be.

*Dear God, help me to earn the respect of
my community. Amen. —ML*

Communication

"Come, let us build ourselves a city, with a tower that reaches to the heavens, so that we may make a name for ourselves; otherwise we will be scattered over the face of the whole earth."
GENESIS 11:4

Communicating can be a difficult task. People can think they are speaking perfectly clearly, but their listeners may be utterly confused. People may think they have full understanding of a message, when they've only got half the point—and that happens even when everyone is speaking the same language!

After the Flood, people moved east. They got together and decided to build a city. But not just any city. A city that would have everyone talking. They wanted to be great. They wanted to be remembered.

So God, our creative Father God, decided to deal with the pride of this people in a unique way. He didn't destroy their building. He didn't take away their tools. He confused their communication.

And the most amazing part of this story is, it worked. The people stopped building the city and were scattered over all the earth. These people who had built a city together—and were on the way to building a tower to reach the heavens—were stopped in their tracks by a lack of communication.

How much could we accomplish if we could only talk to one another a little better? How many parent-child relationships could be repaired? How many marriages saved? How many of us could stay together, instead of being scattered?

Dear God, help us to understand one another better. Amen. —ML

A Poor Substitute

*When the woman saw that the fruit of the tree was good
for food and pleasing to the eye, and also desirable
for gaining wisdom, she took some and ate it.*
GENESIS 3:6

Have you ever eaten half of a double-fudge chocolate cake when what you wanted was a date? Have you ever cursed at another driver when you wanted to get to the hospital faster to see a dying friend? Have you ever bought a new purse you couldn't afford when you wanted to dump some emotional baggage?

The desires weren't bad. The fulfillment of them was inadequate.

Our loving God created us with desires. We desire food, clean air, freedom from pain, understanding, justice, and love. If these desires (and others) are not satisfied, natural consequences result—stomachs growl, our lungs hurt, our bodies deteriorate, we get depressed, etc. Our good God wants our good human desires to be fulfilled. He did not create us in order to watch us suffer.

But every time we try to fulfill our natural desires outside of His plan for us, we'll come up short.

Eve desired food. She wanted knowledge. And she wanted to please her mate. These are all good things. And they are all things God would have loved to give her. But instead, she mistook fruit for fulfillment.

Anytime and every time we replace God with something else—food, career, money, sex, fame, drugs—we will lose out. At worst, our temporary fix could end up destroying ourselves and others. At best, we'll be left with the bitter taste of a poor substitute.

*Dear Lord, help me to always be satisfied by
You—and You alone. Amen. —ML*

Recipe for Idleness

She. . .does not eat the bread of idleness.
PROVERBS 31:27

Among the many wonderful and admirable qualities of the noble wife described in Proverbs 31 comes this one—that she is not a lazy thing but instead looks after everything to do with the running of her household. Or, as the proverb writer put it, she "does not eat the bread of idleness." What exactly goes into a loaf of idleness? Let us consider a recipe.

> ¾ cup flowing gossip (in place of prayer requests)
>
> 1 package ridiculous reality TV shows (watched during "quiet time")
>
> 1 teaspoon snarky Twitter posts (instead of paying bills)
>
> 1½ tablespoons sentimental reminiscing over mementos (preferably added during the time one is supposed to be cleaning out the closet)
>
> 1 tablespoon fat (delivered in form of your choice—potato chips, skipped exercise routines, ice cream, couch time, etc.)
>
> ½ cup Internet window-shopping
>
> 3 cups all-purpose distraction

What would your bread of idleness look like? Are there any ingredients you could trim out of your life? Everyone needs some free time now and then; there's no problem with that. But if your household duties are suffering due to overindulgence in distractions, it might be a sign that you need to reassess your time-management abilities.

Dear God, help me to be a better manager of my time and to balance my priorities. Amen. —ML

Just for Looks

Such regulations indeed have an appearance of wisdom.
COLOSSIANS 2:23

In his letter to the people of Colossae, Paul addresses relatively new believers. He encourages them to continue to build up their faith and to stay focused on the way of Christ, instead of being led astray by popular beliefs of the time or being confused by inaccurate teachings.

Here at the end of chapter 2, he especially warns against getting caught up in rules that might appear to be wise and holy but really are just creations of man and not useful for growing in faith.

There are about as many breeds of Christianity as there are styles of church architecture, and this can be confusing to anyone, but especially to new believers. What would your answer be if a person walked into your city or town and said to you, "I'd like to learn about Christ. Which church should I go to?" Are there some Christians you think of as "true" Christians and others as "not exactly" Christians? What makes the difference?

We need to be careful, when thinking of our brothers and sisters in Christ, not to become arrogant about our own version of Christianity. It's good to be discerning and to think carefully about what the scriptures mean. It's good to think about what is truly wise and what just looks that way. But, at the end of the day, we need to admit that not a single one of us has a perfect understanding of God's Word.

Dear Lord, help me to give as much grace to others as You have given me. Amen. —ML

Confidants

A gossip betrays a confidence,
but a trustworthy person keeps a secret.
PROVERBS 11:13

This is one of those proverbs that states the obvious, right? People who gossip about others are not good choices for your secrets—if they tell other people's secrets, what's to stop them from telling yours?

But the second part of the proverb is interesting. It's easy to imagine that most of us, when reading this verse, immediately distance ourselves from that first person: "a gossip." Nooo, we are most definitely not gossips. But a "trustworthy person"? Are we that?

How good are you at keeping secrets? And what are your guidelines for knowing whether something is a secret or not? For some people, unless you say the words, "Please don't tell anyone," or something along those lines, your words to them are fair game.

Sometimes in our everyday chatting, we forget to keep the Golden Rule in mind. Treat others' words the same as you would want your own words treated. Don't spread around comments made to you in haste or as part of an inside joke that could be twisted if out of context. Don't repeat words spoken in the heat of anger. Don't treat every prayer request as an opportunity for sharing to the world. If you have any doubt at all over whether or not someone would like her words repeated, ask her.

In this way, you will come to be known as a trustworthy person. A person who keeps a secret, and then some.

Dear God who knows all, help me
to guard my words. Amen. —ML

Choice Morsels

The words of a gossip are like choice morsels;
they go down to the inmost parts.
PROVERBS 26:22

The Bible is filled with delicious metaphors. This verse features one of them: "The words of a gossip are like choice morsels."

Isn't that a perfect description of a juicy bit of personal news? When you hear someone tell about a new romance forming between two former enemies, about something scandalous a friend did on vacation, or about something particularly humiliating committed by a favorite celebrity or a respected politician, do you start "salivating" mentally? "Ohmygoodness, wait till I tell _____." The thrill of being able to relate an exciting piece of news is enough to make your heart beat a little faster. It may even give you butterflies in your stomach.

But here is an instance where the King James Version may have a better representation: "The words of a talebearer are as wounds, and they go down into the innermost parts of the belly."

Hmm. Not so exciting. A little sickening, actually. But possibly more like the truth. Words of gossip can be like little bits of food poisoning. The food tastes wonderful in your mouth and fills you up for a while. But soon after, it can cause an illness that knots up your insides and makes you wish you'd never even stepped foot inside the restaurant, much less eaten the food.

Watch out what you choose to consume. You don't want to end up sick.

Dear God, help me consume only healthy words. Amen. —ML

The Source of Meanness

"A good man brings good things out of the good stored up in his heart, and an evil man brings evil things out of the evil stored up in his heart. For the mouth speaks what the heart is full of."
LUKE 6:45

It's so easy to be gracious with people who are nice to us, isn't it? People who do us favors, compliment us, or are just generally polite—we can give them the benefit of the doubt without hesitation.

But a critical person, a bitter person, a hateful or mean person—these we find hard to overlook or understand. It's easy to see them as flat characters—the bad guys. However, no human being is ever that simple.

"The mouth speaks what the heart is full of." And how does a heart get filled? Generally through years of interactions with other humans. If those interactions are mostly good and healthy, full of love and kindness, the words that come out of such a person are more likely to have those qualities. But if those interactions are bad and damaging, full of hatred and bitterness, the words that come out of that person's mouth are more likely to be hurtful and unkind.

So when you come into contact with "an evil man" (or woman), be careful, but also try hard to be as gracious, merciful, and kind as you would to anyone else. You might just get some goodness into that person's heart, causing some evil to be flushed out.

Dear Lord, help me to see people as You see them. Amen. —ML

Clouds without Rain

They are clouds without rain, blown along by the wind.
JUDE 1:12

Beautiful billowing gray clouds on a sweltering hot summer's day are a sign of relief. Rain is coming. The earth will be refreshed, wilting plants will receive a drink, and everyone will get at least a small break from the oppressive heat.

But clouds without rain can be oppressive themselves. They can trap polluted air close to the ground and keep the heat from moving on. A sky full of the unceasing gray, headache-inducing light of cloud cover can be rather uncomfortable.

Jude speaks of some ungodly people in this way. He compares them also to "autumn trees, without fruit and uprooted—twice dead" (verse 12) and calls them "wild waves of the sea, foaming up their shame; wandering stars, for whom blackest darkness has been reserved forever" (verse 13).

Wow. Pretty bad, right? But then a couple verses later we find that "these people are grumblers and faultfinders; they follow their own evil desires; they boast about themselves and flatter others for their own advantage" (verse 16).

That could describe a bunch of people you know, couldn't it? That could maybe even describe ourselves. Grumbling, faultfinding? This is a daily activity for many of us, whether out loud or in our heads. It's an activity that can be headache-producing and stifling—distracting us from our goals and killing creativity.

It's far better to rain down compliments instead of complaints and to provide refreshment to those around you instead of a roomful of hot air.

Lord, let Your sweet spirit rain down on me. Amen.—ML

Our Song

*By day the LORD directs his love, at night his song
is with me—a prayer to the God of my life.*
PSALM 42:8

Think of a song that has special meaning to you. Maybe it's a song that reminds you of a perfect summer spent with a friend. Maybe it's a song that was played at your wedding. Maybe it's your song, the song you and the love of your life have claimed as a symbol of your relationship together.

What is it that you like about this song? What feelings does it stir inside of you?

All through the Bible, we find people worshipping God through song. They sing to God about winning battles and the birth of babies. They sing songs of lament and songs of praise, songs sinking with sorrow and songs bouncing with joy. There is, of course, a whole book devoted just to this exercise: Psalms.

But only one time in the Bible do we find "his song." And His song is a prayer designed for us to give back to Him.

By day God guides us, and at night He still leaves the doors of communication open. What do you think His song is saying to you? What do you want to sing to Him?

*Dear God, help me listen for Your song, and help me find
the words to sing praise to You every day. Amen.* —ML

Wise Testimony

*"I did not believe what they said until
I came and saw with my own eyes."*
<small>2 CHRONICLES 9:6</small>

King Solomon became famous in his time and still is famous. He is known for his great riches, temple building, and many wives, but most of all for his wisdom (though some would say those last two contradict each other).

The queen of Sheba heard of this great king and came to Jerusalem "to test him with hard questions" (verse 1). What she discovered was even greater than the reports. So much so, the record in Chronicles says she "was overwhelmed" (verse 4). She was so impressed by his wisdom, she praised God:

> "Praise be to the LORD your God, who has delighted in you and placed you on his throne as king to rule for the LORD your God. Because of the love of your God for Israel and his desire to uphold them forever, he has made you king over them, to maintain justice and righteousness."
>
> <small>2 CHRONICLES 9:8</small>

When you live a wise life, people notice. If you live wisely for God, people notice God. And that can be a beautiful thing. But it can also make your life a little difficult. As people realize you have a source of wisdom, they'll come knocking on your door more often. And as crazy as it may be, the more you deal with people, the more understanding you gain; and the more understanding you gain, the more you rely on God.

*Dear God, bless me with wisdom, so I
can honor You. Amen. —ML*

Charm School

If a snake bites before it is charmed, the charmer receives no fee.
ECCLESIASTES 10:11

You've known some. Everyone does. Maybe you have been one yourself.

Charmers.

They come with sparkling smiles, twinkling eyes, and all the right words at just the right times. They know which buttons to push for pleasure and how to avoid every hint of pain. They don't necessarily weave lies, but they certainly spin more flattering tales than the pure facts would allow.

Charm can get you a long way. With some people, it can get you a long, long way.

But charm is limited. It's only a matter of time before people come to need some actual, substantive truth. Humans are vulnerable. When real injury comes, a wink and a smile will not make the pain go away. When the snake bites, the poison stings, no matter how beautiful the music was just moments before.

Enjoying a charming conversation is harmless, as long as you remember it is just that—all talk. Do not be so mesmerized by a person's charm that you forget your own weaknesses. And, if you are the charmer, be careful. Don't be so convinced of your own powers that you forget what is the truth. Remember: That snake can bite you too.

Dear Almighty God, help us to rely on what is true and right for all time, instead of what seems good for the moment. Amen. —ML

Our Great Contender

Do not be far from me, Lord. Awake, and rise to my defense! Contend for me, my God and Lord. Vindicate me in your righteousness, LORD my God.
PSALM 35:22–24

Though there have been many great achievements through the work of women fighting for their rights and equality, there have also been some significant downsides.

You've got to stand up for yourself. This is a common refrain heard from women to women over the years—urging women to demand their right to vote, their right to property, their right to be heard, their right to equal pay.

But when did it become a bad thing to ask God to stand up for us? When did we stop relying on God to fight our battles? When did we stop even thinking He could?

Our Lord God is the greatest warrior of all time. He is our Guide, our Leader, our Defender, our Shield. He is all-powerful, all-knowing, almighty, and all good. Why would we ever hesitate to call on Him? Why would we ever think that our own strength could somehow be diminished by being supported by the Creator of the universe?

The next time you find yourself facing a battle, don't wait. Don't try to do it on your own. Don't stand up by yourself. Ask God to contend for you.

Almighty God, please defend me from my enemies, and help me fight my battles. Amen. —ML

The Great Collector

*"Every animal of the forest is mine, and the cattle on
a thousand hills. I know every bird in the mountains,
and the insects in the fields are mine."*
PSALM 50:10–11

If you've ever been around little children in the summertime, you know how they like to make discoveries and collections. They love to capture little bugs and make little homes for them and observe their little bugs' lives. Perhaps children just like to have some things to call their own.

As we grow older, we make collections, too (some of us end up on television shows with whole houses full of them!). Usually these collections don't involve bugs—perhaps jewelry, or books, or shoes. But we love to have things we possess, to call our own. The trouble comes when we start to worry about possessing more things, or losing the ones we have. Or when the possessing of things becomes more important than caring for people.

God's collection trumps all. He is secure in His ownership of all creatures and all things. And as children of God, we are both part of His collection and coheirs of His kingdom. We can neither take pride in owning things nor be afraid of losing what we own. God will take of us. God will keep us. God will supply everything we need. Because He can!

*Dear Lord of all things great and small, please help
me trust in You to provide all I need and to help
me let go of what I don't need. Amen. —ML*

Mentors

*Teach the older women to be reverent in the
way they live. . .to teach what is good.*
TITUS 2:3

The word *mentor* can scare people. They think attending a counseling program or having a degree is required to be one. Or that being under a mentor means you'll be taking a lot of personality tests or doing yoga. Or maybe doing yoga while taking personality tests.

The relationship of mentor to mentee (can someone please think of a better term?—sounds a bit too much like *manatee*) is a long-established and biblical form. Think of Jesus and His disciples. The mentor is a person with experience and wisdom to share with another person. That other person is someone who is willing to learn. It's as simple as that.

The relationship works best when the mentors take their responsibilities seriously. Your words of wisdom will not ring true if your lifestyle does not match up. That's why Paul instructs Titus to teach the older women "to be reverent in the way they live." Only if they have self-control will they be able to reliably "urge the younger women to love their husbands and children, to be self-controlled and pure, to be busy at home, to be kind, and to be subject to their husbands" (verses 4–5).

In Christian communities, this mentoring relationship is hugely important. It can bring a community of believers closer together. By setting up paths of accountability, such bonding can make the whole family stronger and better and, through the development of honorable and admirable lives, more able to be a good witness to nonbelievers.

*Dear God, help me to seek out relationships
that will bring me closer to You. Amen. —ML*

Empty Words

"Everyone will have to give account on the day of judgment for every empty word they have spoken."
MATTHEW 12:36

A glass can be empty for two reasons. Either it was never filled or whatever had been in it was poured out.

Our words can be empty in the same ways. Some words we let fly without thinking. Like an arrow shot up into the sky, these words are aimless and purposeless, yet still able to hurt someone. We never mean anything by these comments, we're just, well, talking. Shooting the breeze. Chitchatting. But all the same, we can sting someone with insults or reveal too much about lives that are not our own.

Other words we may use often and deliberately. But through overuse or misuse, or both, these words have become meaningless. They are promises we never keep, rules we never enforce, feelings unsupported by actions.

But, in the end, these empty words will carry the same weight as those full of meaning. It's a bit terrifying to understand that we will be held accountable not just for the bad things we have said but for the nothing words we have said. "For by your words you will be acquitted, and by your words you will be condemned" (verse 37).

Those not-so-sweet nothings may add up to a whole lot of serious trouble.

Dear Jesus, help me to use words that are true and good, and always to mean what I say. Amen. —ML

For Your Friends

*"Greater love has no one than this: to lay
down one's life for one's friends."*
JOHN 15:13

Fortunately, most of us will not be called upon to die for our friends. But we may frequently be called to lay down our lives for them in smaller ways.

When a friend is going through a time of illness, you stop and offer help, or bring over some healthy soup. When a friend is busy and needs a babysitter, you make room in your schedule to take care of her children. When a friend is nervous about a job interview, you pause in your day to pray.

These are small sacrifices, but it is the faithfulness of these small sacrifices that builds a firm foundation for long-lasting friendship.

Jesus said, "You are my friends if you do what I command" (verse 14). He may indeed ask us to die for Him. But more often than not, He will command smaller sacrifices from us. To speak truthfully of Him. To give a cup of cold water in His name. To visit the sick and those in prison. To love our neighbors. To take care of His sheep.

We are His friends, not just if we are willing to lay down our lives for Him but if we are willing to take up the everyday duties He requires of us and complete them faithfully.

*Dear Jesus, help me to obey Your
commands every day. Amen.* —ML

Above All

*Above all, love each other deeply, because
love covers over a multitude of sins.*
1 PETER 4:8

How deep does your love go?

When we love someone, it's a choice we make. A choice to see a person as the best he or she can be. A choice to keep on going, even when circumstances are rough. A choice to overlook offenses, to forget bad feelings, to forgive.

How deep does your love go?

Does it go deep enough to cover daily irritations? Deep enough to reach past long-ago mistakes and not bring them up again? Does it go deep enough to continue to hang on to promises that will likely never be fulfilled?

How deep does your love go?

Does it go as far as the distance that grows between two people? Does it cover little insults? Does it go deep enough to silence words that should not be said?

How deep does your love go?

Does it go deep enough to trust? Can it cover over deceit? Does it go deep enough to swallow up betrayal?

How deep does Jesus' love go?

Dear Jesus, help me to love as You love. Amen. —ML

Agents of His Kingdom

For you died, and your life is now hidden with Christ in God.
COLOSSIANS 3:3

Have you ever wanted to be an undercover agent? (Perhaps you already are!) To live a secret life? Have you ever just wanted to hide out for a while, to not be known, to go unseen? Have you ever felt like more happens in your own mind than most people will ever know?

Paul tells the Colossians to set their hearts and minds on things above (see verses 1–2). For since they accepted Christ and buried their old lives, their lives are now "hidden with Christ." Once you've been buried with Christ in baptism, your life is no longer just about what you do here on earth. It's no longer about cleaning toilets, riding the subway, or making dinner. Every moment of your life is claimed by Christ—every moment is hidden with Him.

What this means is that what you do here matters. What you do now matters. No one has a full understanding of what life will be like after death, but the lives we live now and the lives we will live then are connected somehow—the core of who we are continues on. For "when Christ, who is your life, appears, then you also will appear with him in glory" (verse 4).

You must keep living and working in this world. But isn't it wonderful to think the real stuff of life is hidden somewhere behind the scenes, kept safe to be revealed in glory?

Dear God, there's so much I don't know or comprehend.
Help me understand You more. Amen. —ML

Like-Minded

Make my joy complete by being like-minded, having the
same love, being one in spirit and of one mind.
PHILIPPIANS 2:2

Paul delivers a heavy dose of practical advice in his letter to the Philippians. If you ever have any trouble with people, go to that book of the Bible and you'll find some helpful ideas on how to better your relationships.

Here Paul presents the concept of "being one in spirit and of one mind." Now this sounds lovely, of course, but how exactly does a person go about achieving this? We are all such different people—some of our friends may be somewhat similar to us in personality and interests, but some are vastly different. And strangers are another story.

Thankfully, Paul gives us some pointers. He says to "do nothing out of selfish ambition or vain conceit" (verse 3). Start there—get rid of your cares about what you alone accomplish. Then, "in humility value others above yourselves, not looking to your own interests but each of you to the interests of the others" (verses 3–4).

If you are putting someone's interests above your own, do you see what happens? You start to try to understand what that other person needs—how she feels about what she wants, and why she wants it. As you place her interests above yours, you start to care more about what she cares about. You start to become more like-minded.

"One in spirit and of one mind." It's a goal worth working toward.

Dear God, train me to see others' needs
before my own. Amen. —ML

Even If He Doesn't

"The God we serve is able to deliver us."
DANIEL 3:17

King Nebuchadnezzar was looking to make a statement. He made a ninety-foot-tall image and set it up on a plain for all to see. Then he commanded everyone within hearing of the official music to fall down and worship the image. Anyone who refused would be thrown into a roaring furnace.

Shadrach, Meshach, and Abednego, followers of the one true God, refused to worship Nebuchadnezzar's idol. They knew what would happen to them for disobeying the king's orders, and they still refused, saying, "If we are thrown into the blazing furnace, the God we serve is able to deliver us from it, and he will deliver us from Your Majesty's hand." They definitely had confidence in their God. Even as they stood before the man who had the power to order their deaths, they did not back down.

But that wasn't all they said: "But even if he does not, we want you to know, Your Majesty, that we will not serve your gods or worship the image of gold you have set up" (verse 18). "Even if he does not."

Have you been praying hard for something to happen recently? Something you really care about? Are you able to pray those words, too: "God, even if you do not. . ."?

Faith in what God can do is one thing. Faith in God that continues even after God doesn't do what you want Him to do requires a lot of guts.

Help me, Lord, to believe even when things don't go my way. Amen. —ML

Joy and Grief

Rejoice with those who rejoice; mourn with those who mourn.
ROMANS 12:15

Celebrating good times together doesn't come that hard to us. Most everyone enjoys a party—at least some aspect of it: free food and drinks, decorations, happy people, party favors. Even if you are sad, it's hard to stay that way if you are surrounded by a bunch of joy-filled people. So the command to "rejoice with those who rejoice" doesn't sound so difficult.

But mourning with those who mourn? This makes us squirm. What do we say? What do we do? None of us likes to feel awkward or ill-equipped. Yet that is often how we feel when dealing with people who are stricken with grief. Maybe we don't like being reminded of our own sorrows. Maybe we don't like being vulnerable.

Maybe we've had bad experiences of our own with people trying to comfort us in times of grief. People say stupid things, ask stupid questions. They talk too much, or neglect to say the only words we want to hear. If we've had these kinds of bad experiences, we at least have some wisdom about what *not* to do.

Mourning with those who mourn doesn't really require much action on our part at all. It mainly requires being able to be still for a while. To sit with someone and hold her hand. To listen. To learn about what the other person needs. To love as you would want to be loved.

Dear God, give me a greater gift of empathy
so I can serve others well. Amen. —ML

Complete Honesty

They did not require an accounting from those to
whom they gave the money to pay the workers,
because they acted with complete honesty.
2 Kings 12:15

The temple was being restored in the time of King Joash. Money had been collected from all the offerings and donations, and from the census and other sources. We aren't told exactly how much money it was, but it was a lot.

The priests were told to hand over the money to the workers who would be restoring the temple so restorers could get on with their work. And so the priests did—bags and bags of it. And the workers took the money and used it for all the expenses related to repairing the damage done to the temple.

And there were no accounts kept. No books watched. No records written down. The priests didn't need to, because everyone performed their duties "with complete honesty."

How different is the situation in workplaces today! Even within the church, people tend to be quite concerned about making sure where every dime is going. And that's not a bad thing. It's good to keep records, collect information, and hold everyone accountable.

But it's also good to be a trustworthy person. To always labor in such a way that no one has to check your work. To be a good manager of your time and resources. To act with complete honesty.

Dear God, help me to trust others and
to be worthy of trust. Amen. —ML

Morning Orders

*"Have you ever given orders to the morning, or
shown the dawn its place, that it might take the earth
by the edges and shake the wicked out of it?"*
JOB 38:12–13

Job is a book filled to bursting with beautiful, lyrical language. The story presented—mostly in poetic form—is about a righteous man named Job, who was used by God to show Satan that no matter what happened to Job, the man would not "curse God and die!" (Job 2:9). It was a test to show that humankind could have faith in spite of circumstances.

Many of us would like to give orders to the morning. Mostly, we would tell it to be quiet and come back in twenty minutes. The image depicted in the verse above comes out of a passage near the very end of the book of Job, where God responds to all He has heard throughout Job's lament of his losses and suffering, and through the arguments between Job and his friends. The Lord listens to all this going back and forth and then speaks to Job out of a storm.

God poses many rhetorical questions, all to show the might and wonder and mystery of the Almighty. In these words are some amazing ideas that really cause us to stop and consider who God is.

And that is what we should do, especially when we face our worst trials. Stop and consider who God is. That no matter what happens, He will not leave us. And that He alone has the answers for us.

*Thank You, God, for providing glimpses
of You in Your Word. Amen. —ML*

Unhealthy Interests

They have an unhealthy interest in
controversies and quarrels about words.
1 TIMOTHY 6:4

Never before in human history has it been so easy to make money from words. Through Twitter feeds and blogs, Facebook pages and websites, radio, television, and podcast talk shows, everyone wants to get her two cents in. And everyone wants to be paid a lot more than two cents.

Any controversy that hits the headlines has to be hashed and rehashed by the talking heads. Sometimes it seems their whole purpose is to get people excited, upset, or angry. They whip up emotions that weren't even there before and magnify the smallest disagreement into something significant.

And. . .it can be fun to watch or listen to. Right? People wouldn't keep making these shows if they weren't so popular. It's thrilling to watch people get caught up in the heat of an argument. The quick-witted exchanges between some opponents can be downright funny, and often the issues they are talking about are real, important moral problems that are of great interest to any caring person.

But let's be careful. It's all too easy to get caught up in controversy to the point that you find yourself spouting malicious talk and harboring suspicions about the "other side" that are not justified. It's too easy to develop an unhealthy interest in quarreling for the sake of quarreling and find yourself dishonoring God and alienating friends.

When in doubt, extricate yourself from the web or turn the channel.

Dear Lord, help me to avoid meaningless
controversies. Amen. —ML

Glue

He is before all things, and in him all things hold together.
COLOSSIANS 1:17

Drop. Break. Creak. Crack. Crash! Have you ever felt like your life was falling apart? Like all the plates you have been spinning are starting to fall, crashing on the ground, pieces flying? Like you haven't just dropped the ball, but you've dropped the whole football field? Perhaps right on top of your family?

It's times like these you wish for some supernatural superglue. Something to stick everyone and every part of the daily schedule back together. Something to make you whole again.

As women—mothers, daughters, sisters, friends—we are often the glue that holds our families together. We keep the household running. We make sure the chores get accomplished, the bills get paid, the appointments get kept. We are the family calendar, the family reminder, the family feeder. So if we start to lose it, everyone loses.

That can be a lot of pressure. We need to know that there is someone who is holding us together, even when we feel like falling apart. Jesus has been with us since the beginning. He is "the beginning and the firstborn from among the dead" (verse 18). He can handle our struggles. And He can put us back together again, even if we let everything fall. There is always hope in Him.

Dear Jesus, thank You for being a friend I can
always count on. Help me remember to trust You
with all the details of my life. Amen. —ML

Biding His Time

When the devil had finished all this tempting,
he left him until an opportune time.
LUKE 4:13

He is clever, you'll have to give him that. The devil waits patiently, looking for that moment when our defenses are down.

Do you know your weak moments? How about what tempts you? One of the best ways to guard yourself from the devil's schemes is to know yourself.

For some of us, our vulnerable time comes, as expected, when we are tired. We've been doing a lot, for a long time, and finally get time to rest. It is then that we have to stay on the alert and make sure our source of refreshment is a good one.

For others of us, our weak moment comes right when we are on top of the world. We'll be in the middle of celebrating some personal or professional achievement, and the devil will come along and whisper to us prideful thoughts, greedy desires, or enticing entitlements.

For some of us, temptation comes in familiar packaging. It's that flavor we love to savor or that store where we love to browse.

For others, temptation comes in the shape of novelty—something new and exciting, something that makes us feel unique, daring, and special.

After being rejected, the devil left the Son of God alone. But he didn't give up. So you can be sure he won't give up on you. But don't let this discourage you. The same Jesus who rebuked the devil in the desert is walking with you every step of the way in your wilderness.

Dear Jesus, keep my heart safe. Amen. —ML

Instruments of Peace

*They will beat their swords into plowshares
and their spears into pruning hooks.*
MICAH 4:3

This beautiful image of weapons of destruction being shaped into instruments of growth comes to us from God's words to the prophet Micah. If you go to the gardens of the United Nations, you can find there a striking bronze statue representing these words (a gift from the former Soviet Union)—a strong man hammering his sword into the blade of a plow.

God was describing a time when the mountain of the Lord's temple would be established, and nations would come from far and wide to have their disputes settled. Peace would reign.

However, peace does not reign without hard labor. That is the beauty of this image. The swords are not just laid down. The spears are not just set aside. They are used for the work of growing new relationships. For digging into the muck and making room for seeds of hope to take root. For cutting off branches that are sick and dying or that are weighing down the tree.

What muck do you need to move to start a troubled relationship on the path to peace? What load do you need to shed? What needs to be cut out of you so forgiveness can happen and new growth begin?

It may not even be your own relationship. Perhaps you have a friend who has held a grudge for a long time. How can we help one another to shape our sharp tongues into instruments of peace?

Dear God, help me be a peacemaker. Amen. —ML

Cleaning Day

A time to keep and a time to throw away.
ECCLESIASTES 3:6

Are you a keeper or a pitcher?

Do you hang on to jar lids, toilet paper tubes, and loose screws because somebody might find them useful someday? Do you religiously keep every award, greeting card, and wedding favor ever received?

Or do you treat clutter with contempt, working diligently to make your house devoid of knickknacks and paper stacks? Do you regularly pitch half-used notebooks and half-remembered mementos?

Keepers, listen up. There is a time to throw away. Pick a room, a closet, or even a drawer, and go through it with these questions in mind: Do I really need it? If I don't keep it and someone needs it two weeks from now, will it be the end of the world? If this burned in a house fire, would I miss it? If your answer is no to any of those, throw the thing away.

Pitchers, listen up. There is a time to keep. Some things are useful, if not for future use, then for future reference. Old letters, old photos, the craftsmanship of those we love and who love us—these are things all too rapidly disappearing from the world. Before you throw something away, ask yourself these questions: Is it valuable to someone in my family? Could I learn something from this? Could this be recycled or made functional for another use right now? If your answer to any of those is yes, don't pitch it, just yet.

Keepers and pitchers, learn from each other.

Dear Lord, help me to know what's most important. Amen. —ML

Unchained Melody

God's word is not chained.
2 TIMOTHY 2:9

Alive, active, powerful. Moving, living, breathing. Able to divide and conquer. Able to build up and encourage. Full of wisdom, full of grace. Thrilling, intriguing, mysterious. Curious and creative. Written, spoken, revealed. To be followed, respected, and desired. Beautiful. True.

God's Word, apart from His Son, is the greatest tangible gift God has given humankind. The fact that we can hold in our hands the very words of God, that we can read them, understand them, and gain knowledge from them, is astonishing. The fact that He trusts us to be keepers, doers, and respecters of His Word reveals more amazing grace than any of us can fathom.

It is an honor and duty to share the Word of God. We cannot keep such a gift to ourselves. "God's word is not chained." It is meant to go, to be told, and to be obeyed.

Paul was willing to "endure everything," knowing that through his experiences, God's Word would be spread and others would "obtain the salvation that is in Christ Jesus, with eternal glory" (verse 10).

What are you willing to endure for the sake of spreading God's Word?

Dear God, help me to share Your great gift with everyone I know. Help me to think carefully about how to do that and then go do it today. Amen. —ML

House Arrest

*"But see, we are slaves today, slaves in
the land you gave your ancestors."*
NEHEMIAH 9:36

Do you live as a free person? If so, do you know where your freedom
comes from? And if not, do you know what's holding you back?

Nehemiah writes about the Levites who cried out to God,
reciting a brief history of the Israelites and culminating with this
statement: "But see, we are slaves today, slaves in the land you gave our ancestors so they could eat its fruit and the other good
things it produces. Because of our sins, its abundant harvest goes
to the kings you have placed over us. They rule over our bodies and
our cattle as they please. We are in great distress" (verses 36–37).

"Because of our sins." Isn't that the snare for any of us when
we are trapped? That is what imprisons us. Our sins.

God had planned for the Israelites to live freely and happily in
a land flowing with milk and honey. He had set aside His chosen
people to rule over other nations in peace and wisdom. But the
Israelites rebelled and rejected God. They set up their own gods
and set their hearts against their Lord.

How much have we missed of what God had planned for our
lives because we've done the same—rejected Him and replaced
Him with our own idols and ideas?

God surely does not want us to be slaves in our own homes. If
you are living as a slave to sin, it's time to be set free. Ask God to
show you the way.

Dear Lord, please set me free from my sins. Amen. —ML

Sacrificial Living

*Therefore, I urge you, brothers and sisters. . .to offer
your bodies as a living sacrifice, holy and pleasing to
God—this is your true and proper worship.*
ROMANS 12:1

The whole system of religious sacrifice can feel a bit foreign. Though we may have read about it in the Old Testament, we still can't quite stomach the idea of killing creatures as offerings to God. To some of us, the practice of animal sacrifice may seem harsh and cruel.

If that is true for you, then human sacrifice must seem completely unfathomable. Yet God asks us to be a "living sacrifice." For some of you, this idea may seem as terrifying as being offered up to a dragon. "What does it mean? And how do I go about doing it?"

Paul tells us what it means and how to do it. "Do not conform to the pattern of this world, but be transformed by the renewing of your mind. Then you will be able to test and approve what God's will is—his good, pleasing and perfect will" (verse 2).

If we renew our minds in Christ, getting to know Him and trying to think like Him, we will become closer to living like the people God created us to be. We will be able to understand God's will for us and be better equipped to do it, day by day, as a daily, living sacrifice.

Dear Jesus, help me to renew my mind in You. Amen. —ML

The Good Hostess

Practice hospitality.
ROMANS 12:13

Some people were blessed with the gift of hospitality. They have an uncanny ability to say and do just the right things to make every single person feel at ease and at home. They are generous with their time and resources, and always willing to offer up their own space for others to use.

But even if hospitality does not come so easily to us, we cannot neglect the exercise. It's a large part of loving our neighbor. So as Paul urged the Romans, we must practice it.

This does not mean that you need to take up baking cookies or learning how to fold napkins into swans. Instead, try practicing the little exercises that combine to make a good hostess. Try to listen more. Observe more. What do you notice about people? What do they like, what are their interests? What do they not like? What do you hear them complain about or request prayer for?

Evaluate your idea of comfort. What makes people feel more comfortable? Generally, if a person's basic needs are being met, that person will feel satisfied. If a person's needs are being met with special attention paid to that person's own particular preferences, that person will feel loved. Give someone a plate of food and he will not be hungry. Give someone a plate of food that is seasoned well and has been carefully chosen based on her dietary needs, and she will be completely filled.

Lord, help me to share with those in need in
ways that show Your love. Amen. —ML

Family First

*Anyone who does not provide for their relatives,
and especially for their own household, has denied
the faith and is worse than an unbeliever.*
1 TIMOTHY 5:8

Sadly, we have all heard at least one story of some person in high standing in a church who has had an affair, committed a crime, or gotten involved in some kind of scandal that has left the family reeling.

The words Paul writes to Timothy in 1 Timothy 5 seem harsh, but they are full of truth. You cannot go about providing for a community, helping others, and giving your time and resources away while turning your back on relatives in poverty. You cannot take care of your neighbors but neglect the people living in your own house.

But how does this make you worse than an unbeliever? Because an unbeliever is under no compulsion to care for anyone outside of themselves. If you are a believer, however, you are commanded by God to love one another—and this command certainly does not grant exceptions for family.

Not only is it a shirking of duty, but you also severely damage your witness to unbelievers. If they see you doing good works but know your family is suffering at home, whether that be financially, emotionally, or spiritually, they will think living under Christ really doesn't make a difference. They will see your life as dishonest and hypocritical and, therefore, be unwilling to trust anything you say.

Make sure to remember that your family members are your neighbors too.

*Dear Lord, help me to love my relatives with the
same love You have shown me. Amen. —ML*

Love the Law

The law of the LORD is perfect, refreshing the soul.
PSALM 19:7

Rules. From the time we first learn the word *no* until, well, the time we die, we have an unsteady relationship with rules.

We are human beings, created by God to do good works. But we are human beings, with the free will to choose not to do anything good at all. And so these two selves are always battling each other. The rules are what help us to see the end goals and steer us in the right direction.

When you get tired of following the rules, read Psalm 19.

This psalm is a love song to the law. Perfect, refreshing, trustworthy, right, giving joy, radiant, giving light, pure, firm, righteous, more precious than gold and sweeter than honey. These are all ways the psalmist describes the law and decrees of God, aka the rules.

If you have not felt this way about the law of God for a while, you may want to ask yourself why. Could it be that you just have kept your distance too long? Is it time to renew your commitment to Bible study? Or maybe you have forgotten where you would be without the law of God. Maybe it's time to take an assessment of your life and be grateful. Thank God for where you are, what you know, and who you have become.

Because none of us would know the way without His law.

Dear God, I praise Your wise commands. Thank You for showing me the way to live. Amen. —ML

Daily Bread

*"Give me neither poverty nor riches,
but give me only my daily bread."*
PROVERBS 30:8

There have been many studies that show the relationship of happiness to wealth. Some reveal that money does make people happier. Others reveal that riches destroy relationships.

One study done not too long ago tried to pinpoint the nature of money to happiness in a more detailed way. It looked at a variety of factors, and the conclusion was that it was not any certain amount of money that made people happier—it was the freedom from want.

In Proverbs 30:9, the writer does not ask God for riches—"Otherwise, I may have too much and disown you and say, 'Who is the LORD?' " He does not ask for poverty—"Or I may become poor and steal, and so dishonor the name of my God." The author knows that the most important part of his life is knowing and following God.

So he asks for daily bread. Enough. Enough to get by. Enough to pay for the basic needs. Enough to keep him and his family fed and cared for.

Do you trust God to provide your daily bread? Would you be happy with just enough?

Give it some thought.

*Dear God, thank You for providing for me. Help me to
rely on You daily for everything I need. Amen. —ML*

He Wrote Them Both

God has made the one as well as the other.
ECCLESIASTES 7:14

When times are good, people offer up praises to God and spread good news to anyone who will stop long enough to listen. They talk about how thankful they are and how faithful God is to bless them in the way that He has. They may remember harder times and talk about how God brought them out of those.

But God is in the extremely hard times too.

When we are experiencing trouble, it's natural to wonder why. And when times of very difficult suffering come, it's common for people to ask God, "Why are You doing this to me?"

We don't ask that question so much when times are good, but we should. "Why are You blessing me, God? Why do anything good for me at all? You know I don't deserve it."

We need to learn to see God's grace not just in what He does for us but in what He doesn't do. And we need to realize that the bit of the world we see is just one small piece of a very large story.

So when we are standing in the middle of the book and the chapter is a sad and dreary one, we need to remember at least these two things: first, there are many pages to come; and second, it is by God's grace we are living this story, good or bad as it may be.

Dear Author of my life, help me to remember
to trust You to write my story. Amen. —ML

Provoked

Her rival kept provoking her in order to irritate her.
1 SAMUEL 1:6

Read those words from 1 Samuel 1:6. Who do you picture in your head when you read them?

Does it make you think of someone from your past—an old enemy who was always pushing your buttons? Or maybe the rival of a friend, whose harassment made you more than once want to go and throw the offending person out of town? Do you think of someone currently in your life, maybe someone who isn't even aware of it—whose voice sets your teeth on edge?

Hannah had a rival. And she couldn't get away from her. Hannah and Peninnah were both married to the same man, Elkanah. But Peninnah had sons and daughters, and Hannah did not. Hannah had no children at all. So Peninnah, perhaps out of jealousy of her husband's love for Hannah, kept harassing Hannah. We are never told a single word Peninnah said. But you can hear her all the same, can't you?

"Oh, children, you look sooo lovely today. It is such a blessing of God to have children." "Children, stay away from Hannah. She must have done something very bad for God to close her womb." "Poor Hannah, don't you think Elkanah would be better off without you?"

This went on year after year.

But the Lord did remember Hannah. He saw her faithfulness and her suffering, and He blessed her with not just one child—but six! Know this: no matter who your rival is, the Lord will remember you too.

Dear God, You know my heart. Help me
to be faithful to You. Amen. —ML

144

Father God

You are the helper of the fatherless.
PSALM 10:14

Some of us were blessed with great fathers. These were men who enriched our lives as role models, trainers, encouragers, supporters, huggers, comforters, and friends.

But others of us did not have this experience. Either our fathers were not so kind or they were simply absent. Yet either by their harsh actions or through their thoughtless neglect, they left just as great an influence on our lives.

Thankfully, we all have a Father in God. And He has promised to be a "helper of the fatherless." The psalmist prefaces this with: "But you, God, see the trouble of the afflicted; you consider their grief and take it in hand" (verse 14). Like the good Father that He is, God does not ignore the cries of His children, but He listens to them and encourages them (see verse 17). And better than any earthly father, He is able to take away our fear "so that mere earthly mortals will never again strike terror" (verse 18).

Everyone needs a father. So if your father was never there for you or is now gone, run to your Father God and spend some time with Him. Let Him heal the places in you that are hurting and give you the confidence that comes from the only Person in the world who has loved you since before the day you were born—and will continue to love you forever.

Dear Father, hear and bless Your children. Amen. —ML

Remember Them

*Continue to remember those in prison as if you were
together with them in prison, and those who are
mistreated as if you yourselves were suffering.*
HEBREWS 13:3

As of 2012, there were close to 2.3 million adults in the US prison system. So many faces. So many men and women. So many moms and dads, brothers and sisters, sons and daughters. And yet so invisible.

They are easy to forget. And some of them would no doubt rather be forgotten. But Jesus tells us not to do that. In His parable of the sheep and goats in Matthew 25, the King blesses those on his right, saying, "I was hungry and you gave me something to eat. . .I was in prison and you came to visit me" (verses 35–36).

Just because people have lost their right to live in society does not mean they have lost their right to live in the family of God.

If you have never been in a prison, just imagine for a moment what it is like. You are never completely on your own. You don't have your own space. You don't have your own schedule. You don't have your own belongings, for the most part. You have to strip in front of others whenever ordered to do so. Even your letters are examined. And every day you do the same exact things, over and over again, without a break. And those are the nice parts.

Imagine if you were the one behind bars. What would you want us to do?

*Dear Lord, help me to have compassion,
and guide me to action. Amen.* —ML

Don't Judge

Therefore let us stop passing judgment on one another.
ROMANS 14:13

One thing there is to love about the Christian church is the way we give one another grace. It's so nice to be a part of a group where no one judges another—where people look at one another through the eyes of Christ. Where you don't ever have to fear being shunned for trivial matters or excluded because of the way you look. It's so pleasant to be free from the worry that anyone is watching your behavior with a critical eye, waiting for you to make a mistake.

Well, it would be nice if all the above were true, wouldn't it?

Sadly, followers of Jesus do not always behave this way. Even though Paul urged us to do so, close to two thousand years ago, we still cannot give up one of our favorite pastimes—judging one another. What is it that makes this habit so impossible to break?

Pride. Anytime two or three of us are gathered in His name, there's more than just prayer that happens. Pride happens. Two or three of us find common ground in the way we do things. Next, we find common ground in disliking the way others do things. And the things we are talking about here are seldom weighty matters of morality—more likely, they are preferences of style in worship, teaching, clothing, and so forth.

We need to kick the judging habit and work on "mutual edification" (verse 19) instead. How about we give it a try for the next two thousand years?

Lord, forgive me for judging others. Amen. —ML

Acceptance

*Accept one another, then, just as Christ accepted
you, in order to bring praise to God.*
ROMANS 15:7

Acceptance must rank pretty highly as one of the most popular words of the twenty-first century, along with its sister word, *tolerance*. Both of these words started to gain momentum in the 1990s, as topics such as bullying, homosexuality, gender identity, and universalism each experienced some spotlight time in Christian conversations and society at large.

But these are not new terms. In his letter to the Romans, Paul told them to "accept one another." But that is not where he ended the sentence. He did not say, "Accept one another no matter when, where, how, or why." He did not say, "Accept everything about one another as good because that's the way you are." He did not say, "Accept one another's beliefs as truth."

Let's take a closer look at what he did say: "Accept one another, then, just as Christ accepted you, in order to bring praise to God." The important part there is "just as Christ accepted you." Christ accepted us while we were yet sinners, but He didn't accept us like that to keep us that way. He accepted us so that through His loving gift of grace, we might be saved from our lives of sin and be able to bring praise to God.

We are to accept one another in the same way. To love one another as we are, but to love one another enough to want to be better so that our lives may bring praise to God.

*Father God, please help me to accept others,
just the way You have accepted me. Amen. —ML*

Jesus' Birth

In the beginning was the Word, and the Word
was with God, and the Word was God.
JOHN 1:1

The birth of Jesus is famously recorded in two of the Gospels, those of Matthew and Luke. It's in those stories that we hear about the shepherds, angels, and no room in the inn.

But the beginning of Jesus is recorded in John. "In the beginning was. . ." That's it. Jesus just was. He was with God. He was God. He was the Word.

Not as easy to make carols up about that story, is it?

But it's a powerful and mysterious story, all the same. It brings up all kinds of questions that are difficult, if not impossible, for us to answer. How is Jesus God and also man? Was He man at the beginning with God, or just God? In the beginning, when He was the Word, did He know He would become a man? Did He know He would save us?

The fact that there are parts of Jesus' story that we cannot understand doesn't need to trip us up. In fact, it should increase our confident walk in Him. For what kind of God would He be if we could understand every part of Him? And what kind of Christmas would it be if there weren't still some mystery?

I praise You Lord, for everything You are—the parts
I know and the parts I don't know. Amen. —ML

Double-Edged

For the word of God is alive and active.
Sharper than any double-edged sword, it penetrates
even to dividing soul and spirit, joints and marrow;
it judges the thoughts and attitudes of the heart.
HEBREWS 4:12

Have you ever been listening to a sermon when something strange started to happen? You feel a little uncomfortable. A little sting and then a little itching—like a mosquito just bit your elbow. You wiggle in your seat. You look up then down. At someone else. Anyone else. You squirm. You sweat. You feel. . .convicted.

The Word of God can do that to you.

It's not just a book written by a bunch of now-dead guys. It's the living Word of God. It's not a string of interesting stories and historical events. It's a source of wisdom and strength.

It is sharp enough to divide thought from thought, to separate good and bad intentions, and to reveal buried motives. Just when you thought you had all your secrets nicely tucked away, a word from the Lord will come out, reach into your heart, and make you face up to your sin. And it won't stop there. It will burn into your brain like a bad song until you can't go anywhere without hearing its refrain again and again. It will make you change.

In fact, the Word of God is so powerful and so penetrating, perhaps to be on the safe side churches should start posting warning signs on the doors.

BEWARE: THE WORD OF GOD MIGHT CHANGE YOUR LIFE.

Dear God, I praise You for the gift of Your Word. Amen. —ML

No Shrinking Violets

But we do not belong to those who shrink back and are
destroyed, but to those who have faith and are saved.
HEBREWS 10:39

In Hebrews 10, the writer does a wonderful job of creating a pep talk on papyrus. He reminds the people of where they have been: "Remember those earlier days after you had received the light, when you endured in a great conflict full of suffering" (verse 32). He commends them on their spirit even during persecution, saying: "You. . .joyfully accepted the confiscation of your property, because you knew that you yourselves had better and lasting possessions" (verse 34).

Then he gives this command: "Do not throw away your confidence; it will be richly rewarded" (verse 35).

What? You have to even say that to these people? They couldn't be timid if they tried!

We are to be like these Christians. To remember who we are. To remember where we've been and what we've been through. To joyfully accept our trials, knowing that something better is coming.

We will not be those who shrink back from the presence of God, afraid to come near Him. We will approach His throne with the security of children of the King—fully expecting His recognition, His identifying us, His grace, and His love.

And because we do not shrink back from God, we will not shrink back from anyone.

Dear God, my King, my Life, my Light—help
me to know for certain who I am and to find
all my confidence in You. Amen. —ML

Mistaken Identity

"Woman, why are you crying? Who is it you are looking for?"
JOHN 20:15

"What does she see in him?" Have you ever asked this question? Some friend of yours joined up with a guy you thought was not worthy of her time, and it left you scratching your head.

Women usually are looking for something in particular when they choose a mate. Some are looking for security. Some for a pleasing physical appearance. Some for reliability. Some for a man who is like-minded or one who is totally different.

And some are looking for a savior.

Mary came looking for the Jesus she had known. Her friend Jesus. Her rabbi Jesus. The Jesus she had seen hanging on the cross, dying.

She came looking for a body in a tomb. She wasn't expecting a living Savior.

So when she saw Him at first, through her tears, she did not realize it was Jesus standing there. Then He opened His mouth and said her name.

Mary almost missed Him. She couldn't see Him for what He was, because she was looking for something else. She was not unlike those women we know—the ones who link themselves with the wrong guy because they can't see reality. They only see what they have been in the habit of looking for.

When we step forward in our relationship with Christ, we should have no doubt about the man we are walking with. He is not a dead prophet—He is a risen King. And when people ask, "What do you see in Him?" you can say, "I see my Savior."

Dear Jesus, thank You for saving me. Amen. —ML

God Knows

*"Do not be like them, for your Father knows
what you need before you ask him."*
MATTHEW 6:8

The "them" in Matthew 6:8 are an interesting crew. Jesus describes them in verse 7, saying: "And when you pray, do not keep on babbling like pagans, for they think they will be heard because of their many words." Jesus is telling the believers not to be babblers. It sounds like people were having trouble figuring out this prayer thing even way back then.

Are there certain people in your church who are known for the way they pray? When Mr. Black begins to pray, the whole congregation automatically sits down, because they know it will be a long one. When Miss Mauve prays, people try not to laugh, because she employs the biggest possible words in her prayers and only sometimes says them right. When Mr. Horace prays, everyone leans forward—he hardly speaks above a whisper.

Jesus wants us to be less concerned with our style of prayer and more concerned with what we say and who we are saying it to.

The pagans go on babbling perhaps because they can't be quite certain who it is they are talking to or what it is they want their god(s) to do. But we have a Father in heaven who is holy and in control. We know who He is, and He knows us. And we do not have to use many words to make our needs known.

We do not pray to offer God information. We pray to offer God us.

*Dear God, thank You for hearing
my imperfect prayers. Amen. —ML*

Carry On

*Carry each other's burdens, and in this
way you will fulfill the law of Christ.*
GALATIANS 6:2

This verse sounds all warm and fuzzy at first. "Carry each other's burdens." We like that part. After all, we've got burdens, and we'd like some help carrying them! Maybe someone could help us with some house repairs or with some financial advice. Maybe we need the car washed or leaves raked. Maybe we need meals brought after a new baby is born or after the death of a loved one.

These are all things we'd be happy to do for one another.

But this may not be the kind of burdens Paul is describing here. Go back one verse and you'll find this: "Brothers and sisters, if someone is caught in a sin, you who live by the Spirit should restore that person gently. But watch yourselves, or you also may be tempted."

Catching someone in a sin and restoring them? Ohhh, no. That is not what we signed up for. That sounds messy and tricky. In fact, it sounds like the kind of thing that might cost us a friend.

But if we are to fulfill the law of Christ—if we are to love God with heart, mind, and soul and love our neighbors as ourselves—then we will be called upon to speak up when we see someone under the weight of sin. It's our duty to lift off her burdens, and it's our privilege to have ours carried as well.

*Dear Lord, help me to be strong enough
to carry someone's burdens. Amen.* —ML

Choose Glory

*A person's wisdom yields patience; it is
to one's glory to overlook an offense.*
PROVERBS 19:11

Not again. Someone is out to ruin your day.

She didn't do the dishes you asked her to do. She took your favorite mug then made a snide remark when you pointed this out. She talked about you behind your back. She laughed at you. She posted an unflattering picture of you online. She stole your idea and claimed it as her own.

You have had enough. After all, this isn't the first time. You'd be totally justified in getting revenge, by anyone's account.

But there'd be no glory in it. And isn't glory what you really want? To be in a state where people honor the way you live and give you respect?

Revenge may taste sweet for a moment, but it has a bitter aftertaste. People may see an act of revenge as mean-spirited on your part. They may not know your motivation. They may even get hurt in the crossfire. Revenge is seldom straightforward.

Don't let someone's thoughtlessness ruin your day or your reputation. Choose patience. Choose turning the other cheek. Choose glory.

*Dear Lord, help me to keep my temper when I'm under attack.
Help me to be patient and to choose glory. Amen. —ML*

Right to Remain Silent

Women should remain silent in the churches.
1 CORINTHIANS 14:34

Maybe you won't believe this, but it seems pretty clear that there are times when women should remain silent.

In his letter to the Corinthians, Paul lays out many, many things happening in the church at Corinth—most of which are not so good. In chapter 14 (it's a looong letter!), Paul talks about order in worship. Taking care to worship God together in an orderly and proper way so no one is left out or overwhelmed but so that each person can be edified by the community of believers.

One of the main issues here is speaking in tongues. He says quite a lot, but Paul's main points about prophesying and speaking in tongues boil down to this: "In the church I would rather speak five intelligible words to instruct others than ten thousand words in a tongue" (verse 19).

This goes for men and women. If you don't have something instructive to say, keep quiet. If what you say won't be understood by most of the listeners, keep quiet. If you are not even sure of what you mean, keep quiet.

Paul especially singles out women here because of the customs of the time, and perhaps because the Corinthian women were in the habit of disrupting services by speaking out of turn. But his main goal is that "everything should be done in a fitting and orderly way" (verse 40).

Sometimes it is right to remain silent.

Dear God, help me to be wise about when to speak. Amen. —ML

Sunset

*"In your anger do not sin": Do not let the
sun go down while you are still angry.*
EPHESIANS 4:26

It's not unusual for people to argue late in the day. We are human beings. Most of us have a good twelve hours or so in us. During that twelve hours we can be productive, polite, patient, professional, and personable. After that, all bets are off.

So when it's been a not-so-wonderful day already, and you are tired and maybe a little hungry, and someone says just the right thing to set you off, it's extremely hard to keep that temper in control.

So you blow up. And the other person responds in kind. And before you know it, you are in a full-fledged, top-volume, highly fueled, grown-up argument.

And the longer it goes on, the angrier you get. And hungrier. And more tired. It's not a good combination.

So what's the solution? And what if the sun has already gone down?

The exact time of sunset here is not the point. Sometimes it may actually be good to go to sleep and give yourselves some space. But the point is, don't let too much time go by before asking for forgiveness (because it's certain there will be at least one thing you need to apologize for) and smoothing out the ruffled feelings.

And whatever you do, don't wake up angry. That could just be downright dangerous!

*Dear God, help me not to let bad feelings fester
but to be quick to say, "I'm sorry." Amen.* —ML

Not That Kind of Fasting

*"Is not this the kind of fasting I have chosen: to loose
the chains of injustice and untie the cords of the yoke,
to set the oppressed free and break every yoke?"*
ISAIAH 58:6

Fasting is a religious practice that goes back thousands of years. People fasted as a way of showing humility before God and as a way of meditating on one's dependence on God. When you fast, you give up something (usually food) that is important to you in order to focus on what you really need from God.

But in Isaiah 58, God told the prophet that the people had got it all wrong. They were fasting as a show. Other than lying in sackcloth and ashes and abstaining from food on the day of fasting, they did as they pleased—taking advantage of their employees, quarreling, and fighting with one another. God wanted something more from His people than just an appearance of humility. He wanted real sacrifice.

It takes real sacrifice to right injustice and set the oppressed free. It takes more than a day of skipped meals or one fundraising event to make a difference. It takes a lifetime of commitment to seeing what is going wrong in the world and working to do something about it. To give food to the hungry, shelter to the poor, and clothing to the naked.

If you are going to fast, do it for the right reasons. And while you are depriving yourself of one thing, slow down and think of all that others are lacking and what you could do about it.

*Dear God, help me not be religious
but be faithful to You. Amen. —ML*

Mind Your Own Business

*Make it your ambition to lead a quiet life: You should
mind your own business and work with your hands.*
1 THESSALONIANS 4:11

Mind your own business. It's a somewhat rude saying, often used
among children, to express annoyance with someone poking his
nose in another person's private affairs. It means something along
the lines of "Get off my back!" or "This is my private stuff—get out!"

But here the motivation to mind your own business comes
because people will be observing your affairs—public and private.

You should take care of your work so no one can say you are
lazy. You should be responsible and honest in your business deals
so no one can find fault with your professional practices. And you
should work hard and diligently so you stay out of trouble and
earn enough to not have to lean on others or be in debt to anyone.

These are all good things for anyone to do, but especially
important for the follower of Christ. Nonbelievers are watching
what you do to see if your beliefs really make any difference. They
want to know, "Does Christ matter?" The way you behave will likely
not be the only factor in someone's choice to follow Christ or not,
but it could be the thing that sets him or her on the right path. In
this way, your "quiet life" can speak volumes!

*Dear God, help me make wise choices so that the way I live my
life may bring glory to You and hope to others. Amen.* —ML

To Get the Prize

Everyone who competes in the games goes into strict training.
1 CORINTHIANS 9:25

Consider two runners. They both aim to enter a marathon.

Runner number 1 isn't too worried. She feels she's in pretty good shape. She's young; she works out at least once a week. She doesn't worry about drastically changing her diet or checking the state of her running shoes. After all, the event is months away.

Runner number 2 started planning for this marathon ages ago. She's in good shape too, but she trains every day. She tries to eat foods that will increase her endurance and strength. She buys new shoes but gives herself plenty of time to break them in. She follows a carefully constructed running regimen, each week increasing her running time slightly.

Who do you think will finish the race with a good running time? And who won't make it across the finish line at all?

We are in the race of life. Time is short, but the days are long. We have a lot to do, and we never know when our life will come to an end. All of us are running to the same finish line. It's important that we run our races in a way that shows we are serious about getting the prize—eternal life with Christ. We need to show that we are running toward something worth sacrificing for. And we need to be prepared for whatever falls in our path—including other runners.

Dear God, please help me "run in such a way as to get the prize" (1 Corinthians 9:24). Amen. —ML

Sibling Rivalry

Whoever claims to love God yet hates a brother or sister is a liar.
1 John 4:20

"Mo-om!" (Isn't it amazing how children can make two syllables out of that word?) You hear the call and you can tell, before even another sound is uttered, exactly what this complaint is going to be about. What she did. What he didn't do. What she said. What he took. Poking, prodding, pushing, shoving, ridiculing, wrestling.

Siblings. It's a beautiful relationship. But sometimes it can look really ugly.

When we accept Christ as our Lord and Savior, we are children of God—loving brothers and sisters in the family of Jesus. But we don't always act that way. Sometimes we can be pretty hateful toward one another. But that is nowhere near acceptable behavior.

God is not going to send us to the "time out" chair, however. He simply says, "If you love Me, you have to love your brother and sister. If you don't, you can't love Me." And if we can't love God, if our love of God will be rejected by Him, we cannot fulfill the most important command: to love the Lord our God with all our heart, soul, mind, and strength.

God, help me be patient with my brother and sister in Christ. Help me to overlook offenses and forgive quickly. Give me eyes to see them as Your children. Amen. —ML

Surprise

*They are surprised that you do not join them in their
reckless, wild living, and they heap abuse on you.*
1 PETER 4:4

The old gang is getting together—what fun! It's entertaining to
see how much people have stayed the same, or not. And you are
definitely on the "not" side.

You've changed. You don't enjoy the same things you used to
do back in the good old days (which really weren't all that good).
You don't have the same interests, goals, or dreams. Because when
you died in Christ, when you realized your life was full of sin and
you desperately needed Jesus to save you, when you said, "I believe
that Jesus is the Christ," your whole life changed.

But don't be surprised if your former friends aren't happy about
the new you. People tend to not like change. And they *really* don't
like change that makes them uncomfortable. That makes them
feel a twinge of guilt. That makes them think too hard about their
own choices.

Be ready for their surprise and dislike. Remember that you
changed for a reason, a really good, eternally important reason.
If you handle the situation well, your friends will respect you,
eventually. You might even be the one surprised at what an effect
your story can have on them.

Dear Lord, thank You for making me a new creation. Amen. —ML

Talking Face-to-Face

I have much to write to you, but I would rather not write with pen and ink; instead I hope to see you soon, and we will talk together face to face.
3 John 1:13–14 NRSV

Facebook, Twitter, texting, instant messaging. Each has its advantages. But all share one big disadvantage. And it is big.

These technologies are wonderful tools for letting everyone know how you are today, commenting on the weather, or showing a picture of the marvelous dinner you ate last night. They are great ways of finding out when someone will be meeting you or where to go for lunch. They are great places to display your children's artwork or catch up quickly with an old friend.

They are not great places to have heated arguments. To express complicated emotions, serious commitments, or humble apologies.

Long-distance communication used to consist of one form, and one form only. Handwritten letters. In a handwritten letter, you can communicate a lot. You can use as many characters as your hand can write without cramping up, and you can take a long time to thoughtfully choose your words.

But even in a letter, you lose something. You lose something big.

When you sit down with someone face-to-face, you don't just hear her words. You see the meaning in her eyes. You hear the tone in her voice. You have a window to her soul.

And that is big.

Dear God, help me to take the time to give proper attention to every relationship I have. Amen. —ML

Sewing Up Broken Hearts

He heals the brokenhearted and binds up their wounds.
PSALM 147:3

Do you remember the first time your heart was broken? Maybe it was a crush who'd let you down or a favorite pet that died too soon. Maybe it was the supposed love of your life who left you for someone else or a family member who betrayed you.

Whatever happened, there's no doubt it hurt. And it left a mark on your heart. It's a mark of sorrow, but it's also a mark of recognition. It's the first time you realized you couldn't trust in someone or something. That trust could be broken.

Our God knows how to heal broken hearts, not just because He shaped ours but because His has been broken too. By us. Every time we reject God and turn to idols, every time we hurt ourselves or someone else, every time we give in to despair, we hurt our Father's heart.

A heart that does not feel cannot be broken. But it also cannot love. And a heart that loves deeply can be wounded deeply. But God is the great Healer. And He knows how to heal deeply.

God searches our hearts and finds the holes. Then He carefully, over time, joins the pieces together—with new love, care, and understanding.

A broken heart will never be the same as an innocent one. It is forever scarred. But with the scarring comes wisdom, and that wisdom can blossom into compassion for others who have been hurt as well.

*Dear Healer, mend the holes in my heart so I
can offer my whole heart to You. Amen. —ML*

An Advocate

"He will give you another advocate to help you and be with you forever—the Spirit of truth. The world cannot accept him, because it neither sees him nor knows him. But you know him, for he lives with you and will be in you."
JOHN 14:16–17

As Jesus was preparing to leave the earth, He tried to comfort His disciples. He told them that He would not leave them alone. The Spirit of truth would live with them and in them. And He would be their advocate.

Anyone who has been in a courtroom knows the importance of advocates. The word *advocate* comes from the Latin word for voice. An advocate speaks on behalf of another person in order to defend her, to plead her case, or to support her.

An advocate is not a cheerleader—rooting for us no matter what happens. An advocate thinks carefully about our situation, analyzes the challenges, and finds out the best way to help us reach our goals.

And that is who we have living in us. Someone who knows all about us and yet is all for us. But that's not all. Jesus says, "The Advocate, the Holy Spirit, whom the Father will send in my name, will teach you all things and will remind you of everything I have said to you" (verse 26).

Our Advocate speaks for us, and speaks to us about Christ. He reminds us of the words Jesus shared with His disciples and all the people He encountered while He was on the earth. And the Advocate teaches us new wisdom.

Can you think of a better farewell gift?

Dear Jesus, thank You for never leaving us alone. Amen. —ML

Shine

> *"Those who are wise will shine like the brightness
> of the heavens, and those who lead many to
> righteousness, like the stars for ever and ever."*
> DANIEL 12:3

Flash! Sparkle! Bling! So much glitz and glitter in one spot—it's dazzling. When the stars of Hollywood turn out for an event, they really shine. Even their hair shimmers, and their teeth twinkle.

It's astonishing to think of all the expense and labor that goes into sending one celebrity down the red carpet. Or how much time and energy is spent afterward talking about what she wore, how she smelled, and who she was with.

Those kinds of stars are undeniably beautiful to behold, but their time in the spotlight is short. Their shine will grow dim, their sparkle will tarnish.

Daniel received a message about the future—he was told that the wise would shine like the heavens, and the ones who led people to righteousness would shine like stars. Not for a moment or two. Not just for a photo shoot. But forever and ever.

The next time you are feeling a little frumpy or gray, a little old and tarnished, thank God for the wisdom you have. Think about the best decisions you made in the past year. Then pick yourself up, put on something shiny (an aluminum foil tiara? a bouquet of silverware?), and take your own photo. Print it out, and write beneath it, "I shine." Then put it somewhere to serve as a reminder that being wise can be beautiful too.

*Dear Lord, thank You for allowing me
to shine with wisdom. Amen. —ML*

Direction

"I know your deeds, that you are neither cold nor hot. I wish you were either one or the other!"
REVELATION 3:15

Have you ever taken a trip with an indecisive person? It's strangely similar to taking a trip with a busload of tourists. Two hundred twenty-nine opinions on where to go, and not a single definitive answer in sight. It's enough to make a person drive off the road, throw a picnic cloth down, and declare exit ramp 43 to be the newest, hottest vacation destination.

Indecision can be aggravating. And hugely wasteful. While you're spending time going back and forth, considering all the angles, shifting, waffling, and being wishy-washy, beaches erode, mountains crumble, and national parks become subdivisions. On the upside, this decreases the number of destination choices.

It's good to be thoughtful and to take time to make decisions wisely. But the key here is to *make* the decisions. And then stick with them. It's no use deciding something only to keep looking back, wondering if another choice might have been better. Do that and you will eventually get nowhere—either by crashing into some obstacle in front of you or by losing your way entirely.

On the path of faith in Jesus, it's especially important to have a clear goal in mind and to stick with it. The destination is eternal life in Christ. Your road map is the Bible. Ask God for guidance, and choose a straight path. He will bless your efforts. Just make up your mind!

Dear God, please guide me every step of the way. I love walking with You! Amen. —ML

What Forever Is Like

" 'He will wipe every tear from their eyes. There will
be no more death' or mourning or crying or pain,
for the old order of things has passed away."
REVELATION 21:4

Just imagine a world with no pain.

There would be no pharmacies. No pills. No medicines of any kind. No doctors, no nurses. No hospitals. No counselors. No therapists. No psychologists or psychiatrists. No couches. No tests. No tissue boxes.

No funeral homes. No cemeteries. No gravestones or hearses. No coffins. No sorrow. No grief. No heartache. No hurt.

Can you imagine it? What would all those doctors and nurses, counselors and coroners, funeral directors and gravestone carvers do? They would have so much time. They might even have forever.

Think of all the time spent in your life crying over trouble, fighting back pain, going to doctors, healing from hurts. What would you do with all that time?

Maybe you would rejoice. Maybe you would praise God. Maybe you would be so full of life, light, and joy that you would glow. Bounce. Shine. Maybe you would do that forever.

And what of all the diseases, germs, wounds, abuse, and depression? What would they do? Perhaps they would shrivel and die. Perhaps they would dry up and go back to some dark hole from which they came. And maybe they would stay there forever.

Dear God, thank You for the hope we have in You.
I want to live forever with You. Amen.—ML

Not Yet

*In your struggle against sin, you have not yet
resisted to the point of shedding your blood.*
HEBREWS 12:4

Dogs are quite clever creatures. And a dog that wants to be free can be very persistent. First he might try barking constantly to draw attention to his plight. If he is tied up on a leash outside, he may strain at his collar, trying to muscle his way toward the gate in the fence—the gate to the freedom that lives just on the other side. He may wriggle, jump, shake, turn, and stretch to the point that his skin is rubbed raw and starts to bleed. But he'll keep at it, until finally he runs free.

How hard have you been working at removing sin from your life? What tactics have you used to avoid temptation? What discipline have you followed to guide your way to freedom?

In Hebrews 12, the writer compares us to children being disciplined by their father. This discipline is a blessing, since it shows us our Father loves us, and it causes us to respect Him. But that doesn't mean it's easy. "No discipline seems pleasant at the time, but painful. Later on, however, it produces a harvest of righteousness and peace for those who have been trained by it" (verse 11).

Keep up the fight. Learn from the discipline. Don't grow tired of working against the evil in your life. Chances are, you haven't yet "resisted to the point of shedding your blood." And hopefully you won't have to. Remember, your freedom is just on the other side of the gate.

*Dear Father, train me with Your loving discipline,
and help me remember to thank You for it. Amen.* —ML

Decrease the Swelling

Knowledge puffs up while love builds up.
1 Corinthians 8:1

Knowledge is like good food. Eaten in small, healthy bites, it is good for the body and helps us grow. But consumed in too-large quantities all at once, even healthy substances can cause us to be bloated and sick.

Some people think that more knowledge will make them better people. The problem is, they think more knowledge makes them better than anyone else, and they feel the need to share this news.

We have to be careful not to mistake the collecting of information for wisdom. Even people with very simple information about the law and love of God can make wise choices that please the Father. Just because they cannot recite the theological arguments for their behaviors does not make those actions any less beneficial.

We also have to be careful that the freedom that comes with knowledge is not used to confuse or hurt others. Some people may have misconceptions about scriptures that have come from inaccurate translations, which have made the rounds for centuries. It's true that it is best to correct such inaccuracies, but it's not necessarily the case that we have to be the ones to correct the world. And in certain cases, if a person who is new to the faith holds some strong beliefs about what is right in God's sight, then we should not flaunt our freedoms that go against these beliefs in some deliberate effort to unsettle that new believer. These are matters that require a delicate touch. Less puffing up. More building.

Dear God, help me to be humble, knowing all
the wisdom I have comes from You. Amen. —ML

Harm for Good

"You intended to harm me, but God intended it for good."
GENESIS 50:20

Joseph's family was unlikely to appear on the cover of *Good Housekeeping* or win the Family of the Year award. His brothers beat him up, left him for dead, then sold him as a slave. Then even after years had passed and Joseph became a great man and forgave his brothers, these men still didn't trust him.

Joseph had every right to be angry. He had every right to throw his brothers into a prison and never speak to them again. He'd been imprisoned himself, he'd been propositioned, he'd been forgotten and betrayed.

He suffered more in his lifetime than any of us ever will. But God remembered him, blessed him, and made him a man of great authority in the land so that he was in the position to make wise decisions and save many people from starvation.

Instead of feeling entitled to apologies, Joseph wanted redemption in place of revenge. In response to his brothers wanting security, he replied, "Don't be afraid. Am I in the place of God? You intended to harm me, but God intended it for good to accomplish what is now being done, the saving of many lives" (verses 19–20).

Maybe you're in the middle of suffering right now, so deep in it you can't possibly see any good. Take encouragement from Joseph's words. You are not God—you cannot see what He sees. Maybe yet there will be some good that comes out of the harm.

Dear God, help me to trust in Your plans. Amen. —ML

Pardon Me?

"Pardon me, my lord," Gideon replied, "but how can I save Israel?"
JUDGES 6:15

Do you have a job to do that seems too big for you? Maybe it seems too big for ten of you—ten of you armed with the very best of modern technology and all the financial resources you could dream of. Have you been banging your head against a wall, trying to figure out how in the world you are supposed to accomplish your task and why in the world God ever chose you to do it?

You and Gideon have a lot in common.

Gideon was an Israelite, threshing wheat in a winepress, when an angel of the Lord sat down under a tree and spoke to him: "The LORD is with you, mighty warrior" (verse 12).

Gideon looked around to see what mighty fighter the angel was referring to. But Gideon was the only one there. "Come again? The Lord is with us? Why are we getting crushed by the Midianites then?"

The angel responded, "Am I not sending you?" (verse 14).

But Gideon didn't get it. "My clan is the weakest in Manasseh, and I am the least in my family" (verse 15). Can you relate? Is there a voice inside of you that says, "I am small, insignificant. I'm not strong, I'm not a good speaker. I have no skills. I can't do this, God!"?

The angel told Gideon, "Go in the strength you have" (verse 14). The only strength this man had was from God.

That's the only strength you have too. Isn't that enough?

Thank You, Lord, for Your strength. Amen. —ML

Grace So Powerful

And God's grace was so powerfully at work in them all
that there were no needy persons among them.
ACTS 4:33–34

This wasn't some magic. This wasn't a miracle, like tongues of fire appearing on people's heads or men speaking in languages they never knew before. This was the grace of God, working through the family of believers.

These brothers and sisters in Christ sold their land and houses, brought the money to the disciples, and the disciples gave it to those in need. Pretty simple system, right? And pretty amazing. It worked out so well that there were no needy persons in their community. Not one.

What would it take for this to happen in one family of believers in our country? Just one? What would it take for one church to work so well together that everyone's needs would be met?

Just a lot of grace.

It takes grace to let go of our own dreams of wealth and security. It takes grace to not fear doing without. It takes grace to be able to give generously, without asking questions and without needing thanks in return from the receivers of our gift. It takes grace to let go and depend on others.

What would it take for us to let this grace work so powerfully among us?

Dear God, rain down Your grace on this community.
And help us to let it do its work. Amen. —ML

Fault Lines

*"If your brother or sister sins, go and point out
their fault, just between the two of you."*
MATTHEW 18:15

The verses found in Matthew 18:15–17 have caused big problems.
People tend to cite this passage as justification for going after
others who disagree with them, do annoying things, or just have
different ideas from the status quo.

But that is a mistake.

For starters, Jesus said, "If your brother or sister sins." We're
talking sin here—doing something that is actually morally wrong,
not just something slightly obnoxious, irritating, or weird. But
morally wrong.

Then look at verse 16: "But if they will not listen, take one or
two others along, so that 'every matter may be established by the
testimony of two or three witnesses.' " This "every matter" part
refers back to Deuteronomy, which is talking about a crime or
offense serious enough to be brought to court. This is no trivial
insult or instance of momentary neglect.

We have to be careful how we handle the Word of God. Here's
the bottom line: If you have a problem with someone, go to that
person first and try to work it out. If you can't work it out, think hard
about what's going on. Is this a serious offense—or just something
you and your ego need to let go?

If we're not careful, we may find ourselves being the one brought
before witnesses!

*Dear Lord, catch me in my pride, and help me
consider my actions carefully. Amen. —ML*

Help Us Believe

"I do believe; help me overcome my unbelief!"
MARK 9:24

Poor Dad. Ever since his son was small, this father had watched the child suffer with seizures. The work of an evil spirit, the fits were severe and sudden—throwing the boy to the ground without warning. And sometimes this meant he was thrown into a fire or into water, nearly killing him.

The father was desperate to save his son. He just wanted his child to live a normal life.

He got his hopes up. Maybe these disciples of Jesus could heal his son? But no. Another disappointment.

Then Jesus came. The boy's father was so exhausted from worry, he didn't sound too confident. "If you can do anything," he said to the Son of the Most High, "take pity on us and help us" (verse 22).

If You can, Jesus. Jesus, *if* You can, make me happy. *If* You can, heal my heart. *If* You can, cure my cancer. *If* You can, save me. How many of us come to our Lord Jesus Christ, exhausted and disappointed, and forget who we are talking to?

Jesus reminds us. "Everything is possible for one who believes" (verse 23).

At this, the poor father felt a surge of hope and shouted out words that every one of us have felt, probably many times. It's a confusing feeling—somewhere between faith and doubt. Somewhere caught up in hope and yet fearing disappointment. "I do believe; help me overcome my unbelief!"

God, this is my prayer. Help me to believe. Amen. —ML

Get Understanding

"Do you understand what you are reading?"
ACTS 8:30

This was Philip's question to the Ethiopian eunuch who sat reading the book of Isaiah in his chariot on his way home. But it could have been asked of any of us.

When you read the Bible, do you understand what you are reading? What tools do you use to get to know God's Word better? How important do you think it is to have a good interpretation of what's going on in the Bible?

The Ethiopian eunuch was an important official in his country, in charge of all the queen's money. But he was not too proud to ask for help. And for him, understanding meant all the difference. After Philip told him the good news of Jesus Christ, the eunuch decided to be baptized on the spot.

If you feel confused when reading any part of scripture, don't be afraid to ask for help. Get a knowledgeable person to read through it with you. Consult some solid reference works. Check out several sources. Then come back to the Word of God and delight in your new understanding.

You never know. A clearer understanding of the story of God might just change your life. It might make all the difference.

Dear God, thank You for the wisdom of scholars and the guidance of good teachers. Help me to find both when I need them so I can understand Your Word. Amen. —ML

Always

"And surely I am with you always, to the very end of the age."
MATTHEW 28:20

Left, then right. Walking up a mountain, step by painful step. You're tired. The events of the last few days have been emotionally exhausting. And your mind is whirling with thoughts too big for mortals to bear.

But then you see Him standing there, and you feel so clear. So peaceful. So happy! The Lord Jesus, alive! You still can't quite believe it—everything He said has come true.

Of course, some still doubt. Some always will. But you are sure this man is the Jesus you know. The Jesus you'd thought you would never see again in this life.

And now here He is, speaking to you. He's winding things down, you can tell. He said He would be leaving soon. But still. . .you can't help feeling sad, and something else. . .homesick.

"Go and make disciples of all nations, baptizing them in the name of the Father and of the Son and of the Holy Spirit, and teaching them to obey everything I have commanded you" (verses 19–20).

You know what amazing things have been done already—you've seen people healed and brought back from death. You know the power of God is here, now. But you feel a little anxious. So much to be done! Am I worthy of this work? Can I do it once He is gone?

But He says He will be with you. Always. And you have to believe Him. Everything He says comes true. You know this will too.

Thank You, Jesus, for "always." Amen. —ML

The Way of the Wind

*"The wind blows wherever it pleases. You hear its sound,
but you cannot tell where it comes from or where it is going."*
JOHN 3:8

A leaf falls into a pond, and ripples silently shimmer away from the landing point, spreading out like messengers headed to the ends of the earth. The light breeze pushes the leaf through the water, spinning it round and round as it floats away, a little golden fairy boat on a murky, mossy sea. You can see the little boat; you can watch it move across the pond. But you cannot see the hand on its rudder, and you cannot see where the boat will put down its anchor.

You see the effects of the Spirit everywhere you go. They are too numerous, too substantial to miss. They are changed lives: lonely souls made into happy family members, timid minds made into challenging professors, quiet voices turned into loud speakers of truth.

The Spirit gives birth to spirit so God's work can be done in us and through us. How it all works is a mystery for sure, but why is easy. Because God loves us so.

And is the Spirit real? That's easy too. Just open your eyes. Put your face in the wind. Can you feel it? Can you hear it? Can you watch it launch golden leaf boats across a still sea?

That's how it is with the Spirit. Thus, it's got to be real.

*Dear God, thank You for the beautiful
mystery of You. Amen.* —ML

In His Hands

*But the pot he was shaping from the clay was
marred in his hands; so the potter formed it into
another pot, shaping it as seemed best to him.*
JEREMIAH 18:4

Wet, gray, slippery hands cover the squishy blob on the spinning wheel. They hover over it, like a mother bird's wings covering her nest. Then slowly, the blob takes shape. First, more of a circle or ball. Then, as the fingers glide over it, forming it, guiding it, the ball grows taller, thinner. The fingers dip into what is now a column, pushing gently into the middle.

The clay dips down, making a cavity inside the shape, a place to hold something good. The hands dip into water then return to the pot, using the fluid to keep the clay soft and pliable. And the wheel keeps moving round and round, steadily providing motion for the art at hand.

The pot is taking shape now and is almost perfect. But a finger drops down, and the clay moves slightly off its center. The wheel wobbles and slows. The pot falls, twists, bends.

Useless. What good is this?

But the hands move again, covering the clay like before. Hiding it from our eyes. The wheel starts up again, and before we can tell what is happening, a pot is born again. This time it has a little bend near the top, a little dip in its sides. A spout.

The wheel slows. The hands rest.

It's a good pot. The potter is pleased.

*Dear Lord, thank You for working my flaws
into something beautiful. Amen.* —ML

Finish Line

I have fought the good fight, I have finished
the race, I have kept the faith.
2 TIMOTHY 4:7

There are some people who plan so far ahead, they actually write out their own obituaries. They want to be sure it will say what they want to be said about their lives, and not say anything else.

What about you? No matter what age we are—whether just starting out in life, nearing the end of life, or somewhere in the middle—we all think about it from time to time: death. What will people say about us after we are gone? What do we want them to say?

Besides writing your own obituary, there's a sure way to get the results you want. Live the kind of life that will be worthy of good words.

Paul felt his life was coming to an end. As he wrote to his friend Timothy, he spoke of this. He was not boasting, he was just giving his status report, as it were. Good fight fought? Check. Race finished? Check (well, almost). Faith kept? Check.

What does your checklist include? What accomplishments make your list? What goals do you want to be known for achieving? What do you want to do, who do you want to become, before your race is finished? Write them down today. Put a check box by each one. Then go and work out your life, faith, and ministry for all you're worth. Godspeed.

Dear Lord, bless the work of my hands and feet. Make
me Your servant so that at the end of my life, I can look
forward to hearing You say, "Well done." Amen. —ML

Is Church Out of Vogue?

*And let us consider how we may spur one another on toward
love and good deeds, not giving up meeting together, as some
are in the habit of doing, but encouraging one another—
and all the more as you see the Day approaching.*
HEBREWS 10:24–25

New generations rise up and ask the question "Why should I bother going to church?" This must be an ongoing problem, however, since even in the book of Hebrews it mentions that Christians had gotten out of the habit of meeting together. But there are good, solid reasons for attending church. One of them is for worship. Singing to the Lord can, of course, be done outside the church, and showing our adoration to God can be done in all that we do. But singing and praising God along with the body of believers radically uplifts the spirit and is a kind of thanksgiving of the heart that works magnificently in a communal setting.

Also, gathering ourselves together with other believers, as well as listening to the pastor's godly exhortations, helps keep us from straying into false doctrines, becoming enamored with cults, or embracing a worldly mindset.

Other reasons to attend church are to be encouraged in our faith by being around other Christians, to learn the teachings of Christ, and to stay accountable. We cannot walk this dusty road alone. That's why in Hebrews Christians are urged to gather together—even if the world tells us it's out of vogue.

*God, thank You for the steady anchor of the
church and the opportunity to fellowship with a
vibrant community of believers. Amen. —AH*

The Grass Is Always Greener

*And the peace of God, which transcends all understanding,
will guard your hearts and your minds in Christ Jesus.*
PHILIPPIANS 4:7

For some people, peace is that pool of water in the desert that always turns into a mirage.

One of the many ways that peace becomes more illusion than reality is through comparisons—when you start looking at someone else's blessings in relationship to your own.

When staring at everyone else's journey, you're bound to stumble on the road. Many times other people's lives appear happier, richer, fuller, maybe even more sanctified by God. When envy settles in, you tend to lose your grateful heart. You lose your way. And Satan is right there escorting you off the path and into a journey you were never meant to take—a fearsome passage you were never meant to walk. One without joy, laughter, hope, or—peace.

Comparisons can mean a slow death of the spirit. The moment you catch yourself with the-grass-is-always-greener mentality, know that it will only lead you astray. So stay prayerfully focused on God and His way for you. Then the peace that passes all understanding will not be a distant mirage but authentic, and yours.

*God, help me to be content and at peace with
myself and the life You have given me. I am unique
and valuable in Your eyes. Amen. —AH*

The Flash of a Camera

"And whoever wants to be first must be your slave—
just as the Son of Man did not come to be served,
but to serve, and to give his life as a ransom for many."
MATTHEW 20:27–28

In a crowd, the flash of a camera always draws attention. People can't help but glance around to see who's getting his or her photo taken. In that situation it's easy to wonder—could it be someone famous, and wouldn't it be fun to meet him or her? It's admittedly a very natural train of thought, but dig a bit deeper and it's easy to find other motivations.

People get starstruck easily, don't they? They are impressed by movers and shakers, wealth and beauty, brilliant minds, and jet-setters. People are wowed by everything but the idea of being a lowly servant. Such a person rarely gets media attention.

Serving others just doesn't pack much glamour, does it? But God's ways are not our ways, and when Jesus arrived He had a different angle on the world. He still saw life from heaven's vantage point, not from an earthbound perspective. His divine mind set—that is, His servant's heart—was about far more than mere altruism. It had to do with matters of eternity. One could say that Jesus took the concept of servanthood to the most profound depth and yet to the highest height of all—His life for ours.

God, impress upon my mind and heart that
serving is not insignificant or pointless but
has infinite, eternal worth. Amen. —AH

Do Not Be Discouraged

*"I have told you these things, so that in me you may
have peace. In this world you will have trouble.
But take heart! I have overcome the world."*
John 16:33

Even in the midst of communing with God and hearing His voice,
the daily onslaught from a sin-laden world can chip away like a
rock hammer at one's faith, discouraging even the most faithful
followers. There may be times when giving up seems like a reason-
able course, especially when prayers appear to go unanswered.

Perhaps your prayer life feels a little like gazing out onto the
calm surface of the sea, but all the while you're thinking that
your mighty supplications should be building and frothing those
waves up into a real storm of answered prayers. But even when
the sea seems quiet—as if nothing is happening—the oceans are
shifting and traveling all around the world. God is also moving,
sometimes just below the surface where we can't perceive it, but
He is ever working things for good.

Remember, God wants His children to have peace and hope.
The Lord declares in His Word that He has "plans to prosper you
and not to harm you, plans to give you hope and a future" (Jeremiah
29:11). The Lord also said, "In this world you will have trouble. But
take heart! I have overcome the world."

Accept His comfort. Live His commands. Embrace His love.

*God, help me to be persistent in prayer even when I
can't see the direct fruits of it. Don't let me give up on
the power of communing with You. Amen. —AH*

The Stones Will Cry Out

Some of the Pharisees in the crowd said to Jesus,
"Teacher, rebuke your disciples!" "I tell you," he replied,
"if they keep quiet, the stones will cry out."
LUKE 19:39–40

What is *praise* exactly? Parents, bosses, and teachers offer words of approval to their children, employees, and students when they've done something noteworthy. But praising God goes beyond that simple act. Praise to the Almighty should be an elemental part of a person's day, not just an act of song on Sunday morning. Praise to God should come from a grateful state of the heart, when one cannot help but bubble up with a song, a shout of admiration, a whisper of homage, or an act of devotion. Praise to God is a tribute from the soul, and it should not be silenced.

When the Pharisees tried to quiet Jesus' disciples from their jubilant exultations, the Pharisees were admonished. In fact, Jesus' reply was quite clear when He said, "If they keep quiet, the stones will cry out."

Christ's simple but impassioned words said it all. Our ovations of the soul are not only welcome and pleasing, but they are also essential to daily living just as air is for breathing. God brought all of life into existence. He is glorious and worthy of praise. When the time is right, let no man, woman, or child be silenced from his or her heartfelt praise!

God, help me grasp the magnitude of Your brilliance and
to give You praise from a sincere heart. Amen. —AH

Oh, to Be Called Blessed!

Her children arise and call her blessed; her husband also, and he praises her: "Many women do noble things, but you surpass them all."
PROVERBS 31:28–29

A woman of God is a woman who will enjoy the love of her children and the thundering praise of her husband. Now those are Mother's Day presents like no other. Better than a fancy dinner out, finer than a big box of gourmet truffles, and more satisfying than a day at the spa.

To be called *blessed* is to be "supremely favored." Those aren't words that get thrown around often today. When the world is swirling and people are striving in their careers, getting ahead, and putting their needs ahead of others in the name of success, to have someone rise up and say, "Many women do noble things, but you surpass them all," well, that is an amazing tribute.

Ambition that becomes all about *you* isn't worth a lot at the end of the day or the end of a life. Applause might come, but the cheers won't be as lasting and soul-satisfying as the praise that comes due to another's selflessness. Such an attitude shines like a cloudless sky and is as welcoming as the scent of rain. A noble life is full of sacrifice, but it is not without reward.

Are you a woman of God—a woman after God's own heart?

Lord, clothe me with an attitude of selflessness and humility. Help me to live a life that blesses the people around me. Amen. —AH

Women Who Loved Well

Charm is deceptive, and beauty is fleeting.
PROVERBS 31:30

Physical beauty and an enchanting personality—that is, being witty, clever, and intelligent—plays well in the theater of life. But when the curtain closes on earth and the bigger stage opens, what value do those qualities have in the footlights of eternity?

What will matter to the people who knew us? Our collections of antiques and tapestries and doodads? The memory of those things will be gone before you can say, "estate sale." Our numerous college degrees, the languages we learned, and that impressive wall of awards are accomplishments, but they won't be able to compare to what is truly lasting.

In the end, it will matter to Jesus, of course, that we knew Him as our Friend and Savior, but it will also matter that while we walked this earthly life, we loved well. That we saw a need and met it. That we smiled when we wanted to frown. That we were handier with a cup of cool water than a witty comeback. That we chased after a lost soul faster than we chased after a good time. That we loved other people as ourselves. Those things will matter a great deal, and with the power of the Holy Spirit, all those things are within our grasp. They are also ours to give away. Fully, freely—and daily.

Heavenly Father, help me to focus on cultivating those qualities and virtues that are lasting and will make an eternal impact for Your kingdom. Amen. —AH

To Be Happy in Jesus

*But the wisdom that comes from heaven is first of all
pure; then peace-loving, considerate, submissive,
full of mercy and good fruit, impartial and sincere.*
JAMES 3:17

This array of human virtues from the book of James points us to wisdom, but the list is daunting, to say the least. And without the Lord's help, attaining these qualities would be utterly hopeless. But this endeavor isn't supposed to be so much a spiritual tug-of-war as a Holy Spirit–powered free fall. It's much easier to be pure, peace loving, considerate, submissive, full of mercy and good fruit, impartial, and sincere if we trust and obey the Lord in all things. Our flesh will fight this course of action, though, since we hesitate to put our whole trust in anyone but ourselves and the word *obedience* offends our sensibilities.

But the book of Psalms tells us again and again to trust in Him. There is no other way to be happy in Jesus, as the glorious old hymn, "Trust and Obey," written by John H. Sammis, reminds us. Here's the first stanza and the refrain to this beautiful song:

> When we walk with the Lord In the light of His Word,
> What a glory He sheds on our way; While we do His
> good will, He abides with us still, And with all who
> will trust and obey.

> Trust and obey, For there's no other way To be happy
> in Jesus, But to trust and obey.

*Jesus, through Your power and kindness, instruct me in the
ways of wisdom that come from heaven. Amen. —AH*

It's All about Priorities

Your beauty should not come from outward adornment,
such as elaborate hairstyles and the wearing of gold
jewelry or fine clothes. Rather, it should be that of
your inner self, the unfading beauty of a gentle and
quiet spirit, which is of great worth in God's sight.
1 PETER 3:3–4

Americans spend over 250 billion dollars on fashion each year. It's a legitimate business, and there's nothing wrong with our wanting to look nice. But when we care more about a wardrobe of designer labels than we do about the poor who live downtown in boxes, then maybe we need to make a few adjustments in our priorities.

How can we readjust those priorites, then, since the temptations to indulge in extravagant and faddish apparel chase us relentlessly? The Bible reminds us that we're not to be mastered by anything. Yet that biblical teaching seems unbelievably challenging when that diamond watch in the display case has our name on it! In matters of frivolous spending, sometimes being accountable to a friend can help. But many times, through the prompting of the Holy Spirit, we know in our hearts when we've allowed something to take a front seat in our lives when it really deserved the cheap seats in the back—with the obstructed view.

Where do your priorities lie?

God, don't allow me to distract myself with petty,
frivolous things but to live my life for Your glory
with a gentle, willing spirit. Amen. —AH

The Grand Illusion

No temptation has overtaken you except what is common to mankind. And God is faithful; he will not let you be tempted beyond what you can bear. But when you are tempted, he will also provide a way out so that you can endure it.
1 CORINTHIANS 10:13

At first, temptation can seem like a beautiful house that we see from a distance—yes, a gorgeous house by a dazzling blue lake. But after we drive up to the house, then go inside, we find that it is only a shell and that the lake water, dirty and full of debris, has made its way into every room and crevice of the house. We find the walls have deteriorated, and the house is a total shambles—that it is ugly and utterly worthless. We find the difference between what we thought it was and the stark reality of what it is to be no less than frightening.

What the world has to offer is a trick of the eye, but it is enticing nevertheless. God does assure us, however, that He is faithful, and He will not allow us to be tempted beyond what we can bear. If we resist the devil he will flee from us (see James 4:7). That is a promise we should take to heart and one we should use whenever temptation arrives with its grand and glorious illusions.

Oh Lord, my Rock, thank You for the safety and strength You provide. Shield me from temptation, and help me to cling to Your promises. Amen. —AH

The Trees That Catch the Storm

*Brothers and sisters, I could not address you as people
who live by the Spirit but as people who are still worldly—
mere infants in Christ. I gave you milk, not solid food, for you
were not yet ready for it. Indeed, you are still not ready.*
1 CORINTHIANS 3:1–2

Once we accept Christ for who He is and we want to follow Him,
we will hopefully grow in our faith and our walk with Him. We will
be able to take in meat like mature Christians living by the Spirit
rather than drinking milk as mere infant Christians who are still
acting worldly.

But progress isn't easy. Think of the healthiest trees that shoot
up from the forest floor—the great oaks that rise above the others.
They stretch toward the sun and spread their branches wide. But
when the storms of life blow through, many times it's those towering
oaks that will catch the brunt of the wind.

The last thing the enemy of your soul wants is for you to grow
in Christ and His wisdom. So expect storms, and be watchful and
ready. But remember too that we can stand strong like the oak
trees. We can know peace in the midst of the gale. For Christ is the
Strength in our branches and the Light that gives us life!

*Jesus, help me to grow strong in the rich, nourishing soil of Your
love and grace. Make me a warrior for Your cause. Amen. —AH*

One Dress at a Time

I also want the women to dress modestly,
with decency and propriety.
1 TIMOTHY 2:9

Modesty is a word that has gone out of vogue in recent years (no pun intended). It's as popular as poodle skirts and penny loafers. Why? Maybe because it conjures up images of women who wear orthopedic shoes and hairnets and outfits that have as much style and shape as a paper bag.

But in recent years society has swung so far the other way that it's, well, kind of shocking. Even girls of a tender age are allowed to stray so far into the "sexy" zone that it makes one wonder if their new "suggestive look" isn't playing havoc with the innocence of their youth. Then there are the miniature skirts—which are just big enough to use as dusting cloths—that are impossible to move in without revealing more than one's personality.

A sensual air has gradually replaced elegance, and many times a come-hither look is sought rather than authentic beauty. As Christians we should show the world how it's really done. How tasteful and attractive a woman can look when dressed well—graceful rather than racy, stunning rather than scandalous. We are to bring Christ's light to the world. This should be done through our witness, and that witness includes all that we wear, as well as all that we believe and profess.

Lord, may Your light be present in every facet of my
life. Help me to avoid those worldly customs that
could be harmful to my witness. Amen. —AH

What to Do with Freewill

"If you do what is right, will you not be accepted? But if you do not do what is right, sin is crouching at your door; it desires to have you, but you must rule over it."

GENESIS 4:7

Oh, to be a robot. It would make life so much easier, but so boring—that is, if we were never able to make a decision on our own. God must have thought it would be boring too—since to force people to do exactly what He wants, to love Him perfectly every second of every day without a choice, well, that's not interesting and it's not love at all. We must *choose* love for it to be *real* love. We must have freewill. And with that simple act—that availability of choices—comes the chance for making a bad decision. We can choose to hate everything, everyone, including God. Or to love everything, everyone, including God.

That's the sheer terror of freewill and the beauty of it.

Every single thing we do every minute of the day involves a choice, and everything has a ripple effect. Everything has consequences. What we eat for breakfast. What books we read, what programs we watch on TV. Where we go, what we spend our time and money on. Sin is always crouching at our door, but with the help of the Holy Spirit, we can ask it to leave.

What will your choices be today?

Holy Spirit, guide me in my decisions. Help me to be wise, clearheaded, and motivated by a selfless love for You and others. Amen. —AH

Polishing up the Halo

"Be careful not to practice your righteousness in front of others to be seen by them. If you do, you will have no reward from your Father in heaven."
MATTHEW 6:1

Some people wear their halos like spiritual fashion accessories. You know, those circles of light that reside just above their heads—the ones that cast a saintly glow about them. Their halos are worn with pride as they tip their heads just so and gaze into the mirror.

And when the halo gets a little tarnished, the wearer polishes it up with a good deed—one they know will get noticed by just the right people at just the right time for maximum benefit to the halo-wearer's reputation. Their career. Their ego.

It's the way of the world but not the way of the Lord. He doesn't want us to practice our acts of righteousness in front of crowds, but quietly. Otherwise, He warns, the showy deeds we parade around will not be rewarded in heaven—the kudos we receive from men will be our full reward. Are you thinking that's a little harsh? It seems severe at first read, but good deeds that are done with our own gain and glory in mind, are they really all that good? Or are they just worn like spiritual accessories?

Remember, no prize on earth can rival the wonders and rewards that God has planned for His people!

Lord, help me avoid the temptation of airing my good deeds to the masses. May they be done for Your eyes and Your glory only. Amen. —AH

He Knew Us in Our Wombs

*This day I call the heavens and the earth as witnesses against you
that I have set before you life and death, blessings and curses.
Now choose life, so that you and your children may live.*

DEUTERONOMY 30:19

So tiny. So precious is that babe in our arms. We want to protect her at all costs. We would lay down our life for that newborn. But why would some people snatch that protection away just because a yet-to-be-physically-born child is on the inside and not on the outside of the womb? Just because the child isn't finished forming yet? Just because society says that convenience is more important than life?

The Lord knew us in our mother's womb. He formed us there in His image. And He has set life and death before us, blessings and curses. We do have a choice, but God expects us to choose a blessing, not a curse, to honor what He's created. What He cherishes. Just as God expected someone to cherish you while you rested safely in your mother's womb.

Yes, God is weaving together those tiny hands that will one day caress your face. Those tiny eyes that will someday look into yours with such love. And that tiny heart that is already beating close to yours. We can choose to hear it too.

We can choose life—God does.

*Father, thank You for blessing us with the opportunity
to experience a precious life growing within us. Help us
to be good stewards of this privilege. Amen. —AH*

Beads on the Loose

The words of the reckless pierce like swords,
but the tongue of the wise brings healing.
PROVERBS 12:18

Have you ever been in a public place when a woman's beaded necklace broke and the little goobers scattered wildly all over the floor? Quite a sight. The beads will inevitably fly willy-nilly, making lots of racket as they bounce and roll under furniture and escape into every nook and cranny, defying anyone to find them.

So it is with reckless words that are spewed in public. Like beads on the loose, the bits of chatter scatter wildly, making lots of noisy racket. The thoughtless words go willy-nilly and cannot be taken back. They hurt instead of heal. They scatter hither and thither, escaping into eager ears and then bouncing on to other ears that come with a set of lips that are happy to repeat what was said. And so, on and on and on—the beads and the gossip just keep bouncing.

In contrast, wise words bring healing. They wear well. They are like a string of fine pearls that will not break. Valuable. Strong. Beautiful. Wise words can be repeated without fear or regret. No apology will be necessary.

What wise words are on our tongues today?

God, remind me of the weight of my words, and
help me to refrain from speaking carelessly. Give me
encouraging, compassionate words instead of words
that could cause pain or anger. Amen. —AH

The Riches of the Spirit

A generous person will prosper;
whoever refreshes others will be refreshed.
PROVERBS 11:25

Farmers are people who gather, but they also know how to sow. They might be wary of taking that bag of seed and spreading it across the field—not knowing if drought, flood, or pestilence will destroy what grows—but with faith, they offer seed back to the ground in hopes that it will bring a great harvest.

Proverbs 11:25 reminds us that when we sow with a spirit of generosity we will also reap that same bountiful crop. To be big-hearted with our fellow man—or woman—will bring in a great harvest. The wealth might not fill our pocketbooks, but it might come in the form of deep satisfaction, a job well done. Or in other riches of the Spirit, which far outweigh monetary gain.

Also, this same verse promises us that if we put our hearts and minds into refreshing others, we ourselves will be refreshed and renewed. Like the joy of having your friend over for tea and a homemade muffin, with the intent of letting her relax, be herself, and enjoy the company of someone who cares. That's one form of refreshment. And when our friend leaves with her shoulders a little less weighted and a smile lighting her face, we feel restored as well.

Who can we bless today with our generosity?

Lord, help me spread the seeds of generosity among
friends and strangers. Thank You for the joy and renewal
that giving freely to others provides. Amen. —AH

Vats of Sticky Grime

Finally, brothers and sisters, whatever is true,
whatever is noble, whatever is right, whatever is pure,
whatever is lovely, whatever is admirable— if anything
is excellent or praiseworthy—think about such things.
PHILIPPIANS 4:8

Hollywood does a good job of bathing our minds in vats of sticky grime—grime that we have trouble scrubbing off later. We're talking nudity, violence, crude humor, foul language, overly dark themes, and immoral conduct with no redeeming values, to name a few.

Stories are a fabulous form of communication and art, whether on the TV, the silver screen, or in a book. They can be educational, refreshing, challenging, entertaining, and inspiring. But when do we know when a story is too worldly for consumption? What you view and read is between you and God, but common sense says that if the program, movie, or book leaves you feeling depressed, dirty, or hopeless, then it probably wasn't a good choice.

We humans are more than flesh and blood. You and I are spirits, and those spirits are deeply affected by everything that we take in. Everything. We learn to protect our children from what they see, so let us be gentle with our spirits as well, and watch and read what will be uplifting.

When we are settling in with our popcorn, maybe a good question to ask ourselves is, "Would Jesus enjoy sharing this movie, book, or TV show with me, or would it offend Him?"

Father, give me a discerning spirit when I'm confronted
with entertainment that might pollute my mind and
spirit with things that displease You. Amen. —AH

Tossed by the Wind

*But when you ask, you must believe and not
doubt, because the one who doubts is like a wave
of the sea, blown and tossed by the wind.*
JAMES 1:6

Some time ago I heard the story about a pastor who asked his congregation to pray for rain, since the area was in a terrible drought. The congregation did pray, but the pastor admonished his parishioners when no one came to church the following Sunday carrying an umbrella. Apparently no one arrived prepared for rain because they didn't have enough faith that God would come to their aid. I'm not sure if that story is real or not, but it sounds characteristically human. Doesn't it?

That story reflects much of our prayer life. We pray. We have faith—at least a mustard seed's worth, anyway. But then we go on about our business as if nothing will change. Perhaps we've seen a lot of unanswered prayers over the years, and we've become discouraged. But God always listens, and He always answers our prayers. It's just that God responds to our requests from the vantage point of omnipotence, not human frailty.

Yes, we've all had doubts, and when they come, we do feel like we're being tossed to and fro on stormy waves. But Jesus is the Great Rescuer. If we ask Him, He will calm that sea of fear and those terrible waves of doubt.

Ask and believe. . . .

*Jesus, I give You my doubts, fears, and insecurities. Thank You
for hearing all of my prayers— great and small. Amen. —AH*

Not a Pretty Sight

A gentle answer turns away wrath,
but a harsh word stirs up anger.
PROVERBS 15:1

We've seen it a hundred times. Someone—let's call her Lucile—is at the back of the line, and that line isn't budging. First, Lucile might merely frown over the inconvenience, but after a few more minutes of no movement, she starts tapping her foot and cocking an eyebrow. Then if too much time passes, emotions flair hotter so that Lucile is now firing barbs loud enough for the person behind the counter to hear.

When Lucile finally arrives at the head of the line, she is hot enough to poach an egg.

Now, if the person behind the counter responds to Lucile with a sharp retort, there's bound to be a firestorm of wrathful snorts and fiery insults. It won't be a pretty sight.

But now let's back up and imagine this—that same woman behind the counter responds to Lucile with genuine patience and love. It'll be like pouring water on a campfire. You can almost hear the blaze sizzle into smoke. That is the way of Proverbs when it says, "A gentle answer turns away wrath, but a harsh word stirs up anger."

Let us all pray not to be Luciles but the woman who's wise enough to give that gentle answer.

God, give me patience in times of frustration and gentle words
for everyone I meet. Be present in my every action. Amen. —AH

Expect a Miracle

He replied, "If you have faith as small as a mustard seed, you can say to this mulberry tree, 'Be uprooted and planted in the sea,' and it will obey you."
LUKE 17:6

The faith as small as a mustard seed. If you've never seen a mustard seed, you will be relieved to know that you almost need a magnifying glass to see it. Truly, we are all capable of having that much trust in God. That amount of faith is one of the Almighty's tender mercies, since He knows humans have trust issues.

So even with only our mustard seed of faith planted securely in our hearts, we should expect miracles, knowing they come in all shapes and sizes. Some are big, like a hurricane that is diverted back into the ocean. But sometimes we witness smaller miracles, like the reconciliation of friends. And then there are the interventions that at first don't look like miracles at all—like the student who was forced to attend the college at the bottom of her list, only to discover four years later that God gave her the perfect education for her chosen field.

Yes, not every miracle uproots a mulberry tree and plants it into the sea. Some come quietly, like the marvel of the berries on that same mulberry tree, sweet and juicy enough to make jam, pie, and a host of good things to eat and enjoy. After all, isn't that in itself a divine wonder?

Lord, thank You for Your intervention on our behalf—even when our faith is only the size of a mustard seed. Amen. —AH

Stamping Our Little Feet

[Love] does not dishonor others, it is not self-seeking,
it is not easily angered, it keeps no record of wrongs.
1 CORINTHIANS 13:5

We've all known strong-willed children who stamp their little feet and make their whole world—including you—tremble. Well, what happens when that strong-willed child grows into a strong-willed adult? She could become that dreaded coworker who has to be right, all the time, no matter what. She has to have the last word, the final say, and correcting you is her full-time pursuit.

In other words, the child has grown up to be a zealot with a pile of meaningless causes. Her corrections don't rise from righteous indignation but from a prideful need to feel superior.

Could this zealot be *us*?

Many times gotta-be-right folks are clueless that their bulldog approach to interpersonal communication is more biting than beneficial.

Instead of insisting we are right, we can bring in some godly light. We *can* make sure *our* attitude is pleasing to the Lord. That we do not dishonor others. That we are not self-seeking. That we are not easily angered or keeping a record of wrongs. These precepts will help to soften an obstinate constitution, even if we find that the strong-willed child is us.

Heavenly Father, help me to exhibit a pure, selfless love and
to resist the urge to correct and criticize. May my presence
be a soothing balm for everyone I encounter. Amen. —AH

Who Can Resist?

*"Take my yoke upon you and learn from me, for I am
gentle and humble in heart, and you will find rest for your
souls. For my yoke is easy and my burden is light."*
MATTHEW 11:29–30

Your heart is weighted and weary with all the cares of the world.

Now imagine a golden pond lit by the last warm rays of the
sun. The water ripples to the shore, and you sit back and rest
on the grass. You listen to the songbirds until you hear someone
approach. You rise up and see Jesus. He's come, intent on spending
some time with you.

He sits down next to you by the shore. You both say nothing for
a moment as you just enjoy each other's company and the sounds
of the sighing earth all around you. Then you hear Him speak for
the first time, and He says, "Beloved, take my yoke upon you and
learn from me, for I am gentle and humble in heart, and you will
find rest for your soul. For my yoke is easy and my burden is light."

You rise up and smile, for you know in your heart that Jesus is
the answer you've been searching for your whole life.

And you can't resist His ways or the love in His eyes a moment
longer.

*Jesus, thank You for the rest and peace You offer
to those who take up Your yoke. We were created
to love and be loved by You. Amen. —AH*

Something's Dead in the Road

Jesus said to her, "I am the resurrection and the life. The one who believes in me will live, even though they die; and whoever lives by believing in me will never die. Do you believe this?"
JOHN 11:25–26

You're driving through the neighborhood on a spring day with the sunroof open. Your favorite music is playing, and the breeze is ruffling your hair. Oh yeah. You think, *Wow, life is sweet. . .like a dew-covered rose blossom.*

Then suddenly, in that glorious moment, you're accosted by the sight of a dead squirrel in the road. To make matters worse, the poor thing is being picked to pieces by a turkey vulture! Your whole body threatens to go into convulsions.

The day is no longer springy, sweet, or dewy. Instead, a dark cloud shadows the moment. You are reminded that this fallen world is embalmed with the sinful residue of Eden.

Ever since Adam and Eve, life has been a little like something dead in the road, and the enemy has tried to pick us to pieces. It's so terrible our whole body threatens to convulse. What can we do? Well, we latch on to God's hope like there's no tomorrow. We take His Word to heart. Jesus said, "I am the resurrection and the life. The one who believes in me will live, even though they die; and whoever lives by believing in me will never die."

Jesus is asking me. Jesus is asking you. "Do you believe this?"

Sweet Savior, don't allow the hopelessness of this world to discourage me. I choose to believe in Your saving power. Amen. —AH

Creatures of the Night

There is neither Jew nor Gentile, neither slave nor free, nor is there male and female, for you are all one in Christ Jesus.
GALATIANS 3:28

Prejudice can creep around in our spirits like a creature of the night—like a dirty little rat that enjoys the twilight where it can remain hidden from the light. Some people are obnoxious and vocal about their bigotry. Others smile on the outside while they hate on the inside.

It's not easy to love people who don't look like we do. And it may not be fun to celebrate our cultural differences. However, to call ourselves Christians and to live in harmony—it's the only way. Without love on the inside as well as the outside, there will be only turmoil and strife, and it will have far-reaching consequences as it ripples through families, neighborhoods, and cities, and across the world.

Prejudice is more than just a politically incorrect way to live—it's a sin. The Bible reminds us that in God's eyes we are all the same, and like a good father, God loves us equally. We should listen to His words and offer no shadowy places in our hearts for that creature of the night—racism—to hide. Ask Christ to shine His light into every corner of our hearts.

Our spirits may at first squint at the sudden bright light, but we will rest in the joy that comes from a clean heart.

Lord, help me to view everyone—no matter their race or social status—through eyes of love and acceptance. Amen. —AH

Got Wisdom?

*To slander no one, to be peaceable and considerate,
and always to be gentle toward everyone.*
TITUS 3:2

Have you ever met someone who loved a good quarrel? She is the kind of person who will trample over a good time just to hunt down a discrepancy in the conversation—like a hungry lioness after an unsuspecting bunny. When she finds it, she'll go for the jugular, and then everyone cringes at the emotionally grisly sight—the conversational carnage. We've all met a few of those folks, have we not?

First, let's look at the phrase—*a good quarrel.* It seems like an oxymoron. Is there such a thing as a good quarrel? A good discussion, yes, but quarreling isn't celebrated in the Bible. Far from it.

So this argumentative person you know—who has a bumper sticker that reads, I'D RATHER BE QUARRELING—has some serious issues. If you were able to sit back and watch an episode of her antics, it would almost be funny. But not quite. This person takes issue with everything. She wakes up in the morning with her fists up, ready for a verbal battle, and she doesn't put them down until she's sound asleep at night. It's obvious what this woman needs—wisdom.

Wisdom tells us to calm down. To listen more and talk less. To not make our point so sharp that it jabs at someone's heart! Let our new bumper sticker be—GOT WISDOM?

*God, give me restraint and consideration when I interact
with friends, family, and strangers. Amen. —AH*

Fudging through Life

Such are the paths of all who go after ill-gotten gain; it takes away the life of those who get it.
PROVERBS 1:19

It may start with a sheepish grin, because we know what we've done. We fudged on our taxes, but only a little. We pulled the wool over the eyes of the insurance company with some fraudulent maneuvering, but they don't deserve our honesty, since we know all adjusters are really shysters. We took a few "unused" supplies from the company we work for, but it doesn't matter since no one will miss them, and anyway, we got cheated out of that raise we sooo deserved.

"I'm no thief," we may say. "I'm just balancing the scales of justice!"

But any unlawful gain is thievery, and any ill-gotten profits or dishonest dealings will, in the end, bring us more grief than glory. Now why is that—especially if we get away with it, and it seems to bring justice to all parties? Because God is watching, and as long as we're on this earth He expects us to obey the law. One of the Ten Commandments is, "You shall not steal" (Exodus 20:15), and that includes from the government, insurance companies, and our employers.

Why does any of this matter? Because God calls us to be holy, and how can we lead in the great things if God cannot trust us even in the small?

Lord, help me remain faithful to all of Your commandments, even the ones that seem small or inconsequential at the time. Amen. —AH

Wolf in Sheep's Clothing

Do not set foot on the path of the wicked or walk in the way of evildoers. Avoid it, do not travel on it; turn from it and go on your way. For they cannot rest until they do evil; they are robbed of sleep till they make someone stumble.

PROVERBS 4:14–16

There's something frightening about a human being who sets out to do evil and, in the process, drags his friends along. Devious folks hope to entice you away from your morals, and they want you to partake in their dark deeds. Why? It gives the evildoers the illusion of approval. Perhaps they feel if they can spread the blame around they will in some strange way minimize their own guilt. Just as Eve gave the forbidden fruit to Adam.

But all this "party" mentality does is lead other people into a trap. One can almost hear the snap of the metal jaws biting down on the feet of joiners, ensnaring them in a cage of malice. Whether in Bible times or on the rough streets of a modern-day city, Proverbs has it so right when it says that wicked people cannot rest until they do evil. They can't sleep until they make someone stumble. How sadly true no matter the era.

When you experience this person's persuasive words and the path he or she lures you into, what can you do? Flee. Don't hang around to be romanced. The Bible says to avoid this road. Turn from it, and go on your way.

God, give me the wisdom to see a snare laid at my feet and the strength to resist its temptations. Amen. —AH

All the Lonely People

Be devoted to one another in love.
Honor one another above yourselves.
ROMANS 12:10

Even in the midst of a bustling crowd, loneliness can enter a person's heart as easily as rain seeping into the earth. It might show up at Christmastime when everyone is supposed to be cozy at home with family or out on merry outings with friends. It might invade the lives of successful people, the homeless, ministers, and factory workers. And loneliness can infect every part of one's life, including one's health.

John Milton wrote, "Loneliness is the first thing which God's eye named, not good." The Almighty understood that man shouldn't be alone. That we were made for fellowship and friendship.

As Christians, let's keep an eye out for those lonely souls, the people who need a smile and a helping hand. Those who need a cup of cool water and a listening ear—who need a friend. Let us open our hearts and homes to them. As the book of Romans reminds us, "Be devoted to one another in love. Honor one another above yourselves." This is God's cure for all the lonely people.

Amazingly enough, when we reach out to lessen someone else's lonesomeness, perhaps we will ease our own.

Father, give me the desire to live my life for You and for everyone around me. Deepen and enrich my relationships with family and friends. Amen. —AH

A Heart of Gold

A person who's donning favoritism at a party stands out like a pig in a tutu. That person—we'll call her Jane—explodes with gushing adoration when she sees you, but after sixty seconds of "catching up" and "can't wait to hear all your news," she's already peeking over your shoulder. Jane is trying to be subtle. You hope she just needs something from the buffet table, but it becomes obvious what she's up to. Jane's keeping her options open. She's looking for someone more important to talk to—besides you.

Perhaps the new person to enter the room has more money, more connections, more clout, more gifts, more of everything that Jane wants, so she makes her excuses and dashes over to the new arrival.

It is so easy to be found guilty of the transgression of favoritism. Everyone at some time or another has chosen unwisely and put selfishness ahead of wisdom.

But God doesn't look at the outward appearance. He looks at the inside. And for good reason. So if two dinner guests offer themselves—the rich man with the gold ring and the poor man with a heart of gold—who will you choose?

*Holy Spirit, convict me when I'm showing partiality in a
desperate, selfish attempt to feel included and important.
I want to live life by Your standards, seeing through the
exterior and straight into the heart. Amen. —AH*

Lies Are Like Rabbits

"You shall not give false testimony against your neighbor."
EXODUS 20:16

Lies are like rabbits—they multiply until the little rascals are hopping all over the place. Until they can no longer be herded or contained. They are on the loose and ready to proliferate. Again. Except that lies are not as cute, cuddly, and innocent as bunnies.

It's easy to believe that lies are okay if no one gets hurt and we don't get caught, but that idea is in itself a falsehood. Lies always hurt someone, even if it's just our own spirit. And no matter how much we try to fool ourselves into believing that no one knows of our deceit—God knows. He heard it all. And His opinion matters the most.

We may think that lies get us out of a tough corner, but in reality they are a trap, and only the truth can set us free. Then when people find out about our dishonesty—and many times they do somewhere down the line—not only does it grieve others but it can damage our reputation. It will compromise our integrity and our Christian witness. How will people ever want to hear what we have to say about Jesus if what we've said in the past is riddled with duplicity? How can anyone trust us again?

So the next time a lie tempts our spirit and teases our tongue, let's remember that image of all the rabbits on the loose.

*Lord, even if it's painful to do so, let my mouth
always speak the truth. Amen. —AH*

Turning Bondage into Balance

It is for freedom that Christ has set us free. Stand firm, then, and do not let yourselves be burdened again by a yoke of slavery.
GALATIANS 5:1

We can all spot a perfectionist a mile away. She's the gal who's meticulously scrubbing the corners of her house with a Q-tip while the rest of the house is dirty enough to raise petunias. Why? Because it's impossible to perfect everything all at once no matter how hard she tries. The perfectionist will risk ill health to push herself beyond the bounds of reason. Perfectionism is not only dangerous physically but mentally and spiritually as well.

Yes, to strive for excellence is commendable, but to never be able to complete a task or ever feel satisfied by one's work is bondage. And when we can't follow through with the work God has given us to do, it means the enemy has won.

The Lord wants us to have a sound mind, which means finding balance in life. How can we be warm, giving, creative, fun, and a light to the world if we are frozen solid in an unmovable block of perfectionism? Let Jesus melt the block of bondage that says, "Never good enough," and let us be able to shout the words, "It is good, and it is finished. Praise God!"

Lord, help me not to be a slave to perfectionism, but in all things, let me find balance and joy. Amen. —AH

We Were Meant for More

"For I know the plans I have for you," declares the LORD, "plans to prosper you and not to harm you, plans to give you hope and a future."
JEREMIAH 29:11

Have you ever noticed the way ducks seem to struggle to walk on land? They have this injured-looking, toddling thing going on that looks as painful as it does comical. But the moment those same awkward ducks hit the water, their feet and legs suddenly work better. They are gliding like feathers floating on the breeze. That's because ducks were meant to glide.

We too scuffle along on this fallen earth with our toddling, gangly spirits. Every day is a struggle, as if we don't fit on this earth. That's because we were meant for so much more. We were meant to glide in God's glorious presence, not strain with these sinful feet of clay.

The good news is that God still has a plan for us even with our awkward feet and our tottering ways. His plan is to prosper us. Not to harm us. He plans to give us a hope and a future. Remember His promises, and have faith. He will help us find our way if we ask Him—since we were not meant to stumble on sin but glide in His grace!

Lord, thank You that You have a plan for me, a hope and a future. Show me the way—Your way. Amen. —AH

The Time Is Now

But God demonstrates his own love for us in this:
While we were still sinners, Christ died for us.
ROMANS 5:8

Jesus could have chosen a thousand other ways to redeem us. But He chose the most personal, the most meaningful. The most painful, the most beautiful. The one that was all about love.

Jesus chose to be born here and to walk among us so that He would know firsthand the pinch of our hearts when sadness comes, feel the salty tears that splash down our cheeks, and know our great losses and sufferings. But most of all, He came to make us right with God.

Jesus chose us. He chose you. Have you responded to this magnificent offering of Him? In the book of Mark, Jesus said, "The time has come. . . . The kingdom of God has come near. Repent and believe the good news!" (1:15).

Have you embraced this good news? The kingdom of God has come near to you. Why are you waiting? The time is now. Ask the Lord for forgiveness, and be free. Believe in Him as Lord, and be made right with God. Accept His grace, and live with the Lord for all time. Oh, yes, what a joy—to know love the way it was meant to be!

Thank You, Lord Jesus, that even while I was deep in my
sin, You gave up your life so that I might truly live. What a
sacrifice. What a Savior! Thank You for Your unfathomable
mercy, Your immeasurable love. Amen. —AH

Gentle Giant of a Scripture

*"Blessed are the peacemakers, for they
will be called children of God."*
MATTHEW 5:9

Conflict is a necessary ingredient for a good novel and an exciting drama. But conflict isn't a healthy, satisfying, or biblical state in which to live our daily lives. Eventually, a steady diet of turmoil and strife will make us sick in mind, body, and spirit.

Our ongoing life story should be one of peace. This gentle giant of a scripture—"blessed are the peacemakers"—isn't easy to fulfill in a world that craves trouble, hate, and war like a highly addictive drug. But peace should still be our goal. Why? Because our Lord made it a point to mention its import while He was here. Jesus, of course, didn't always choose peace. Let's face it. His earthly presence did stir things up. A prime example was when Jesus turned over the tables of the moneychangers when they were desecrating God's house. The key thing to remember here is that His reaction didn't spring from His ego or pride but from a strong moral obligation to do what was right. Big difference.

If we wake up with strife furrowing our brows, we might ask ourselves, "Where does it come from—my human ego or pride, or a violation of God's values?"

"Blessed are the peacemakers" would not only make a lovely cross-stitch to hang on our wall, but it would also make a lovely motto to reign in our hearts.

*Oh Lord, may I always have discernment and
know how to live a life of justice, as well as be an
instrument of Your peace. Amen.* —AH

God Does Not Reside in a Box

For the LORD Most High is awesome,
the great King over all the earth.
PSALM 47:2

God doesn't reside in a box, but we are so tempted to put Him in one. The Almighty is omnipresent, all-knowing, and invincible. He can create anything, do anything. Sometimes people may argue that God no longer works with visions, dreams, healings, and wonders as He did in Bible times. But do remember: He is the Creator of the Universe—the Great "I Am." He can work His glory in any way He chooses. Yesterday, today, and tomorrow.

We cannot confine the Lord to the limits of our imaginations or within the vantage point of our finite knowledge of the supernatural world. Since God made all things, He has everything at His disposal. Every drop of rain. Every grain of sand. Every beat of every heart. He is the master of all and can use any method or medium He chooses to bring about His plan. There is no box large enough, beautiful enough, or creative enough to house God. As it says in Psalm 68:35, "You, God, are awesome in your sanctuary; the God of Israel gives power and strength to his people. Praise be to God!"

God, may I strive to know You as You really are
and not as I want You to be. May I never limit Your
power in my life, for You are a holy and awesome
God of infinite power and might! Amen. —AH

The Wear and Tear of Daily Life

Trust in the LORD with all your heart and lean not on your own understanding; in all your ways submit to him, and he will make your paths straight.

PROVERBS 3:5–6

The wear and tear of daily life can be exhausting when we're relying on our own wisdom and power. During those trying times we may feel like a beaten-down gopher in one of those games you find at a kids' pizza place. He's the poor varmint that gets beaten with a mallet every time he pops his head up. It happens over and over and over again.

It can be that way in life. And after a few thousand whammies, our spirit gets pretty mangled. We want to scream, "This isn't fun. Turn the machine off. We want out!"

What to do?

The only thing that works is to trust in the Lord, confident in His power, wisdom, and plan. If we trust our own understanding, we're going to get whammed by life. Our perception is so limited, it's like we're trying to see the whole vast earth through a keyhole. Impossible.

If we submit to the Lord daily, our paths will be made straight. That sounds so simple—and it is. But the hard part is that we are a fiercely independent folk. We like doing it our way, as the old song goes. But that self-centered, prideful mode only leads to more wear and tear on our spirit. Let us make life simple again. Trust fully. Submit willingly. Live well.

Lord, help me to trust You daily in all things. Amen. —AH

Stuck in the Past

To the Jews who had believed him, Jesus said, "If you hold to my teaching, you are really my disciples. Then you will know the truth, and the truth will set you free."
JOHN 8:31–32

We are the product of our pasts; people cannot change. Have you ever heard that hopeless summary of humanity? It's a prevalent theory, but the Bible teaches just the opposite.

The truth is that we do not need to keep thrashing along in the dirty old ruts we've created. With Christ, there is a new road. We do not have to be ruled by our past transgressions, our genes, our environments, or our parents' sins. We should dismiss the idea that we will always be overweight. Always struggle with addictions. Always have a short fuse. Always live in debt. Always quarrel with our relatives. Always_____. (You fill in the blank.)

John 10:10 says, "The thief comes only to steal and kill and destroy; I have come that they may have life, and have it to the full."

So denounce the destructive lies of the thief, Satan. Embrace the truth of Christ and live a free and abundant life. Be all the beautiful things God intended you to be!

Holy Spirit, help me to fly free of my past and become the woman of wisdom You intended me to be. Amen. —AH

How much better to get wisdom than gold, to get insight rather than silver!

PROVERBS 16:16

About the Authors

Bestselling and award-winning author **Anita Higman** has over thirty books published (several coauthored) for adults and children. She's been a Barnes & Noble "Author of the Month" for Houston and has a BA degree, combining speech communication, psychology, and art. Anita loves good movies, exotic teas, and brunch with her friends.

Marian Leslie is a writer and freelance editor. She has lived in southwestern Ohio most of her days, but has ventured far and wide through the pages of many good books.